The Test Tutor

Preparation Workbook
for the

WISC®-V Test

Test Tutor Publishing, LLC

TABLE OF CONTENTS

TABLE OF CONTENTS

The WISC†-V Test Explained

The Wechsler Intelligence Scale for Children®-Fifth Edition (WISC®-V) is a testing instrument used by psychologists and institutions to assess intelligence in children ages 6:0 to 16:11 years. Many private and public schools require the submission of WISC-V test results for school or gifted program admission. Generally, the test can be administered within 40 to 70 minutes, and many of the subtests can be administered on an electronic device. The test is comprised of 21 subtests: 10 are primary; 6 are secondary, and 5 are complementary (see chart below). The following table lists the primary, secondary, and complementary subtests.

Primary	Secondary	Complementary*
Similarities	Information	Naming Speed Literacy
Vocabulary	Comprehension	Naming Speed Quantity
Block Design	Picture Concepts	Symbol Translation
Matrix Reasoning	Arithmetic	Delayed Symbol Translation
Figure Weights	Letter-Number Sequencing	Recognition Symbol Translation
Digit Span	Cancellation	
Coding		
Visual Puzzles		
Picture Span		
Symbol Search		

Not included in this workbook

Generally, the primary subtests are used to determine the Full Scale IQ score (FSIQ). The secondary subtests may be used to provide additional information or may be substituted for a primary subtest. Because the choice of subtest is at the discretion of the examiner, this workbook contains exercises for all of the primary and secondary subtests. The complementary subtests are not used to determine the IQ score. Rather, they are used to assess children for learning disabilities or cognitive impairments.

The primary and secondary subtests are grouped into five categories based on the cognitive function they assess: Verbal Comprehension, Visual Spatial, Fluid Reasoning, Working Memory and Processing Speed. The following table lists the subtests by category.

Verbal Comprehension	Visual Spatial	Fluid Reasoning	Working Memory	Processing Speed
Similarities	Block Design	Matrix Reasoning	Digit Span	Coding
Vocabulary	Visual Puzzles	Picture Concepts	Letter-Number Sequencing	Symbol Search
Information		Figure Weights	Picture Span	Cancellation
Comprehension		Arithmetic		

How to Use the Workbook

Each chapter of this book contains descriptions of the subtests, details about scoring, and instructions on how to administer the exercises. Thoroughly read each chapter, walk through the exercises, and make sure you gather all the required materials before sitting down with your child. You will need a stopwatch or clock for timing and a pencil to record your child's answers.

Materials Needed:
- Preparation Workbook for the WISC®-V Test
- 9 two-color blocks (blocks must be purchased separately)

Tell your child you are going to play a series of games with him and that he can take breaks as needed. During the exercise administration, if your child answers more than three questions in a row incorrectly, he/she may need a brief rest or may need to move on to a new activity. If so, feel free to proceed to a new subtest and finish the previous subtest at a later time.

Additionally, for optimal results when administering the test, praise your child's efforts and encourage your child to do his best independently. Once the practice exercises are completed, evaluate your child's strengths and weaknesses.

Information

Description

During the information subtest your child will be asked to verbally respond to various questions about subjects in everyday life. Each correct response given within 30 seconds will receive 1 point.

Instructions

Ask the questions listed below. Try to elicit specific responses. If your child's answer is incomplete ask him "What do you mean?" or "Can you tell me more about that?" Begin by saying: **"Now, I'd like to ask you a few questions. Okay?"**

Question	Answers
1. Show me your hand.	(holds up hand)
2. Name something you drink.	Any consumable drink
3. Name a food.	Any food
4. How many fingers do you have?	10
5. What body part do you use to hear?	Ears
6. What day comes right after Friday?	Saturday
7. What month comes right after October?	November
8. How many legs does a dog have?	4
9. Name a kind of flower.	Daisy, Lily, Rose, Tulip, Violet, etc.
10. What kind of an animal is a sparrow?	Bird
11. Name a planet in outer space.	Mercury, Venus, Earth, Mars, Jupiter, Saturn, Uranus, Neptune
12. Name a musical instrument that people blow.	Saxophone, clarinet, flute, etc.
13. What happens to water when you heat it?	It boils
14. How many seasons are in a year?	4
15. How many minutes are in an hour?	60
16. What are gloves made of?	Fabric, cloth, material, leather, wool, cotton, etc.
17. In what season do the leaves fall?	Fall/Autumn
18. What do people use to talk to each other when they are in different locations?	Telephone, fax, email, letter, Internet, etc.
19. What body part digests food?	Stomach

Question	Answers
20. What body part circulates the blood?	Heart
21. What is an oak?	A type of tree
22. What is a fault line?	A place where two Teutonic plates meet, that when shifted cause earthquakes.
23. Name a famous landmark in Egypt.	Great Sphinx of Giza, Great Pyramid of Giza
24. How many people live in Asia?	Asia's population is about 4.4 billion - the greatest in the world.
25. What is the part of the Earth's atmosphere that blocks the sun's UV rays?	Ozone
26. Who is Leonardo da Vinci?	The artist that painted the Mona Lisa.
27. Tell me the directions of a compass.	North, South, East, West
28. Name a shape with 6 sides.	Hexagon
29. What measures atmospheric pressure?	Barometer
30. What measures air temperature?	Thermometer
31. What happens to a dinosaur bone when it stays in the ground for many years?	It becomes a fossil.
32. What is Newton's law of universal gravitation?	Isaac Newton developed the law that states that a particle attracts every other particle in the universe using a force that is directly proportional to the product of their masses and inversely proportional to the square of the distance between them.
33. What is Photosynthesis?	The process by which plants return oxygen to the air
34. What is Oxidation?	The chemical reaction between objects and oxygen that causes food to rot and metal to rust
35. What is Evolution?	The theory of natural selection developed by Charles Darwin
36. What is Chlorophyll?	The substance that makes leaves green
37. How many continents are in the world?	7
38. Name a famous Chinese philosopher.	Confucius, Laozi, Zou Yan, Mencius
39. How far is it from New York to London?	3,459 miles or 5,567 kilometers
40. Where is the Earth's highest point on dry land?	The summit of Mount Everest in Nepal.

Vocabulary

Description
The vocabulary subtest is administered in two parts: picture and verbal.

Picture Items **(for ages 6 to 7)**
Your child will be shown a picture and be asked to name it. He/she will be given 1 point for each correct answer.

Verbal Items **(for ages 6 to 16)**
Your child will be asked to define words that the examiner reads. Each answer receives 2, 1, or 0 points depending on its accuracy and specificity.

PICTURE ITEMS

Picture Item Instructions (pp. 10-28)

This subtest is administered only to children ages 6-7 years.
Because this subtest simply requires your child to identify objects, the best way to prepare is to make sure your child can identify as many objects as possible. The next exercise includes 114 pictures your child should review and be able to identify.

For each exercise, simply ask the question: **"What is this?"** If the answer is unclear, encourage your child to elaborate by asking "What do you mean?" or "Can you tell me more about it?" The answers are on page 29.

Verbal Item Instructions (pp. 32-34)
This subtest is administered to children ages 6-16 years.
Simply read the question and write down your child's response.

1

2

3

4

5

6

7

8

9
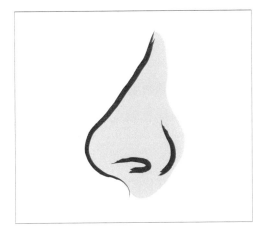

10
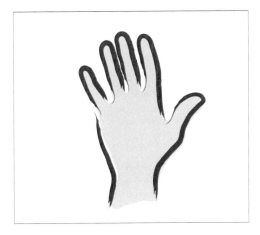

11
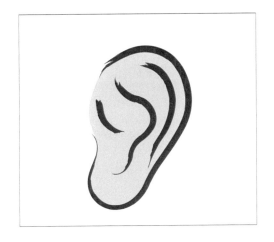

12

13
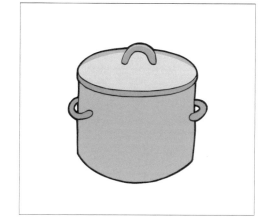

14

15

16

17

18

19

20

21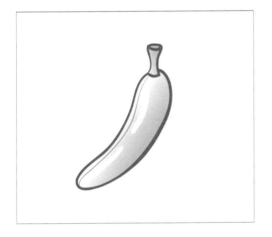

22

23

24

25
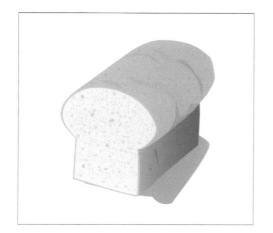

26
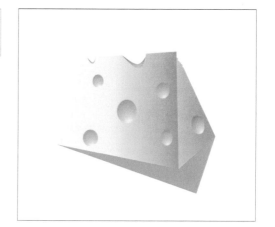

27

28

29

30

31

32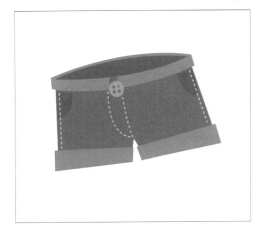

33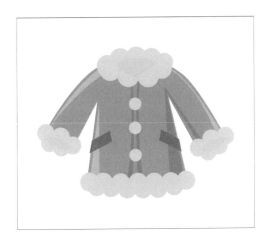

34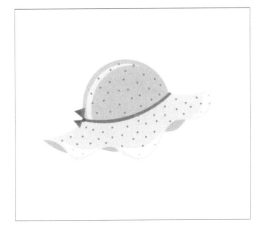

35

36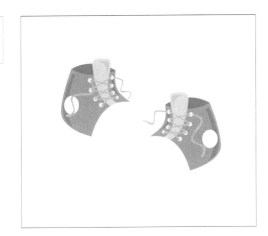

37

38

39

40

41

42

43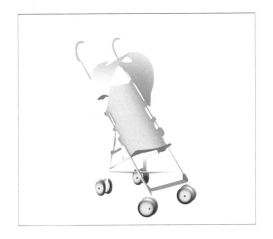

44

45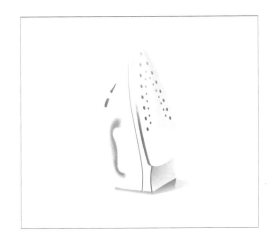

46

47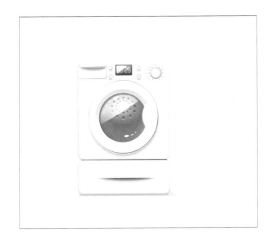

48

49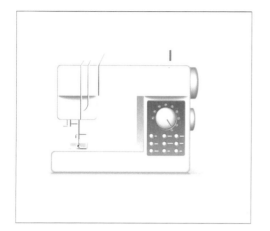

50

51

52

53

54

55

56

57
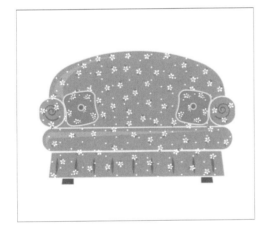

58

59
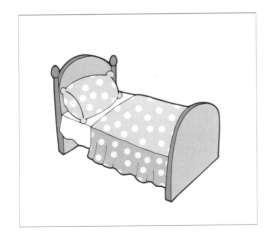

60

61

62
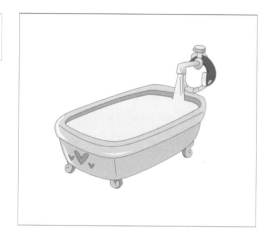

63

64

65

66

67

68

69

70

71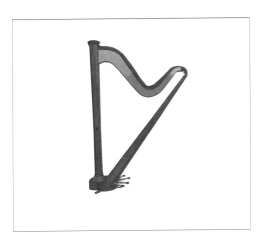

72

73

74

75

76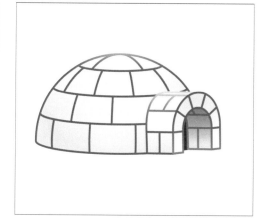

77

78

79

80

81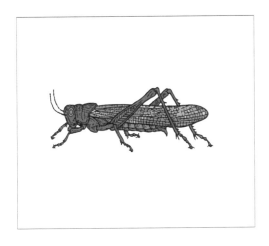

82

83

84

85

86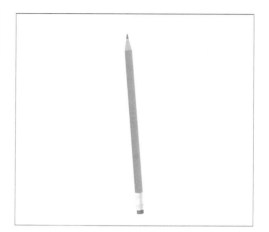

87

88

89

90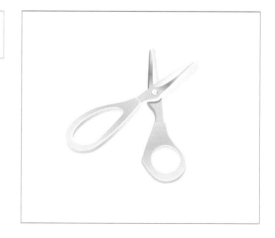

91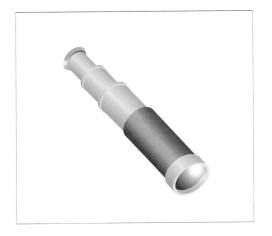

92

93

94

95

96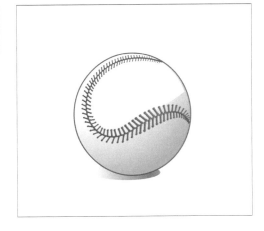

97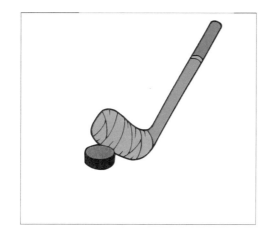

98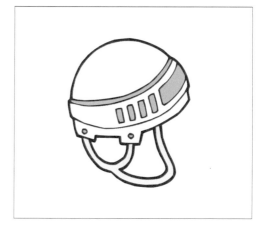

99

100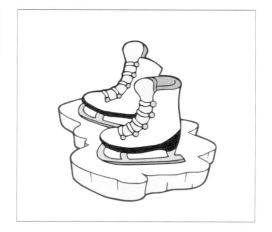

101

102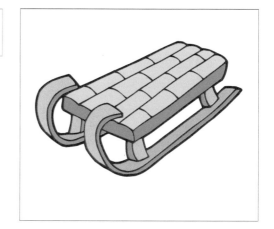

103

104

105
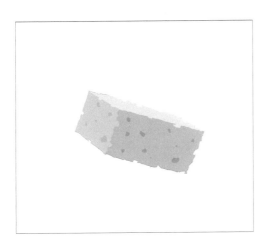

106
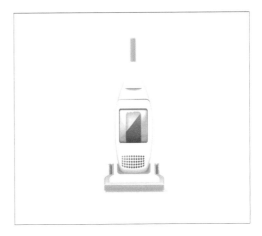

107

108

109

110

111

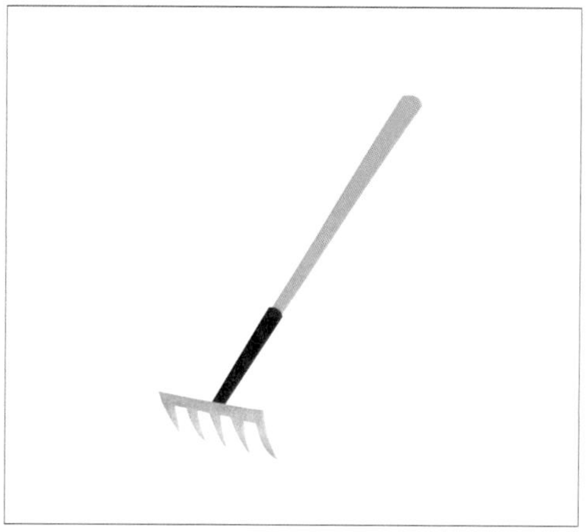

112

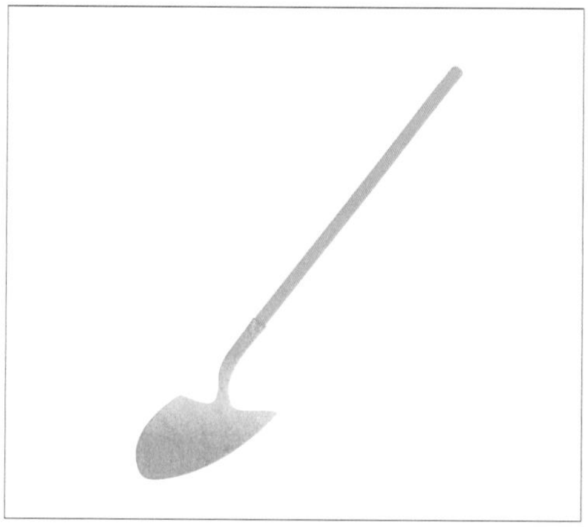

113

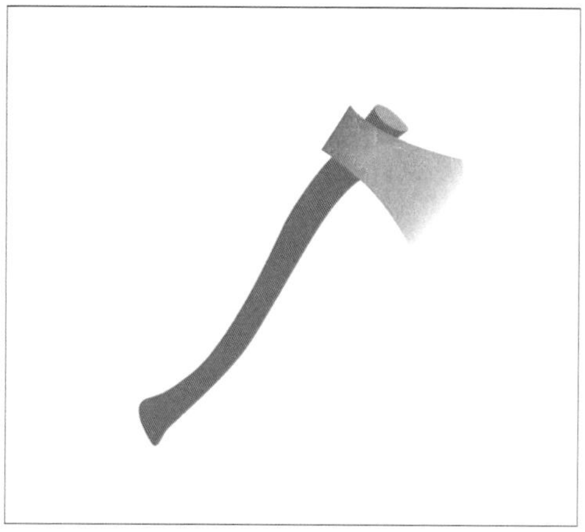

114

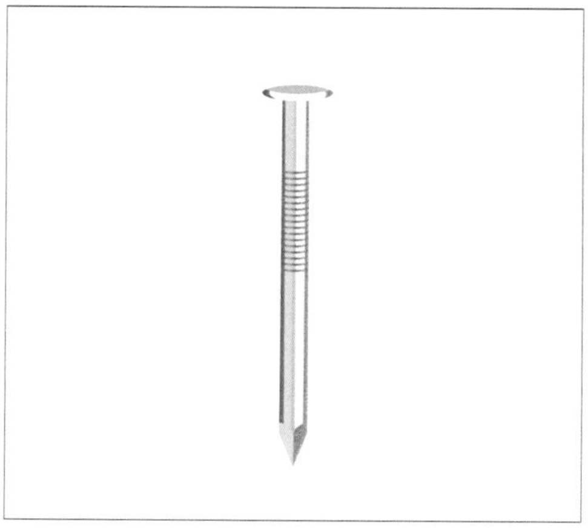

Picture	Answer
1	Cat
2	Dog
3	Cow
4	Duck
5	Turtle
6	Chicken
7	Mouth
8	Eye
9	Nose
10	Hand
11	Ear
12	Finger
13	Pot
14	Pan
15	Glass
16	Teapot
17	Plate
18	Cup
19	Strawberry
20	Apple
21	Banana
22	Grapes
23	Carrots
24	Pumpkin
25	Bread

Picture	Answer
26	Cheese
27	Chicken (meat)
28	Hamburger
29	Cupcake
30	Donut
31	Shirt
32	Shorts
33	Coat
34	Hat
35	Dress
36	Shoes/Sneakers
37	Car
38	Taxi
39	Airplane
40	Bus
41	Bicycle
42	Train
43	Stroller
44	Clock
45	Iron
46	Fan
47	Washing Machine
48	Stove
49	Sewing Machine
50	Hourglass

Picture	Answer
51	Lamp
52	Key
53	Shopping Cart
54	Cash Register
55	Television
56	Chair
57	Sofa/Couch
58	Bookcase
59	Bed
60	Table
61	Sink
62	Tub
63	Crane
64	Bulldozer
65	Tractor
66	Digger
67	Drum
68	Violin
69	Guitar
70	Piano
71	Harp
72	Cymbals
73	Flower
74	Tree
75	Tent

Picture	Answer
76	Igloo
77	Castle
78	House
79	Ladybug
80	Bee
81	Grasshopper
82	Spider
83	Snail
84	Butterfly
85	Ruler
86	Pencil
87	Globe
88	Microscope
89	Calculator
90	Scissors
91	Telescope
92	Crayon
93	Magnifying Glass
94	Football
95	Tennis Ball
96	Baseball
97	Hockey Stick & Puck
98	Helmet
99	Soccer Ball
100	Ice Skates

Picture	Answer
101	Basketball
102	Sled
103	Microphone
104	Newspaper
105	Sponge
106	Vacuum Cleaner
107	Broom
108	Mop
109	Lock
110	Hammer
111	Rake
112	Shovel
113	Axe
114	Nail

Instructions

HINT: Your child should study these vocabulary words and look up their synonyms in a thesaurus.

Say: **"Now I'd like to play a word game. I'm going to ask you what some words mean. Let's start with Watch. What is a Watch?"**

1. What is a **Watch**? (something you wear that tells time)

2. What is a **Cap**? (a head covering; like a hat)

3. What is **Detergent**? (a cleanser, used for washing)

4. What is a **Dog**? (an animal that barks and has a tail)

5. What is a **Motorcycle**? (a vehicle with 2 wheels that you can ride)

6. What is a **Bathroom**? (a place where you take a bath/shower)

7. What is a **Glove**? (clothing to keep your hands warm)

8. What is a **Rat**? (an animal; rodent)

9. What is **Courage**? (bravery; fearlessness)

10. What is an **Award**? (something you get for winning a competition)

11. What is a **Burglar**? (a thief; a robber)

12. What is an **Aviator**? (a pilot of an airplane)

13. What does **Comply** mean? (to obey; to do as you are told)

14. What is a **Nuisance**? (an annoyance; a pest)

15. What is an **Isle**? (a small piece of land that is surrounded by water on all sides; like an island)

16. What does **Imitate** mean? (to copy; mimic)

17. What is a **Myth**? (a fable; a fairytale)

18. What does **Exact** mean? (precise; accurate)

19. What does **Translucent** mean? (clear; see through; transparent)

20. What does **Consumable** mean? (able to be eaten)

21. What is a **Law**? (a rule that is written to protect people from harm)

22. What does **Infrequent** mean? (rarely; seldom)

23. What does **Venerable** mean? (old and respected)

24. What is a **Consensus**? (when everyone agrees on something)

25. What does **Arduous** mean? (physically tough to do; strenuous)

26. What does **Nimble** mean? (moving quickly and lightly)

27. What does **Predict** mean? (to see into the future; foresight)

28. What does **Impending** mean? (about to occur at any moment; imminent)

29. What does **Nearsighted** mean? (able to see things that are close better than things that are faraway)

30. What is a **Modification**? (a change to fix something; a revision or amendment)

31. What does **Verbose** mean? (talking too much; garrulous; loquacious)

32. What does **Coerce** mean? (to force or compel someone to do something)

33. What does **Archaic** mean? (no longer in use; obsolete)

34. What does **Laggard** mean? (slow and pokey; dilatory)

35. What does **Specific** mean? (stated explicitly or precisely)

36. What does **Thrifty** mean? (economical; prudent; frugal)

37. What does **Balderdash** mean? (nonsense; foolishness)

38. What does **Repair** mean? (to fix something that was broken)

39. What is a **Champion**? (a person who saves people; a hero)

40. What is an **Audience**? (a group of people who watch or listen to something)

41. What does **Courteous** mean? (to be polite; to have manners)

42. What is an **Assistant**? (a person who helps)

43. What does **Calm** mean? (quiet and still)

44. What does **Patient** mean? (willing to wait)

45. What does **Amazement** mean? (great surprise)

46. What is **Midnight**? (12 o'clock at night)

47. Who are **Guests**? (people who are visiting in another house, restaurant, or hotel)

48. Who is a **Stranger**? (someone you don't know)

49. What does **Unusual** mean? (something that is different; not seen every day)

50. What is a **Vacation**? (a time to relax away from home)

51. What does **Overjoyed** mean? (really excited about something)

52. What is a **Transformation**? (a change in how something looks)

53. What is a **License**? (permission granted by the government to do something or own something)

54. What does **Enormous** mean? (very big)

55. What are **Diamonds**? (highly valued precious stones made from heated coal)

56. What is an **Invention**? (a new creation that makes our lives better)

57. What does **Amiable** mean? (friendly and approachable)

58. What is an **Anomaly**? (an abnormality; irregularity; aberration)

Comprehension

Description:
During the comprehension subtest, your child will be asked general questions about societal and social norms, rules, and consequences. Answers are given 2, 1, or 0 points based on accuracy and specificity.

Instructions:
Begin this subtest by telling your child that you are going to ask some questions and you want him/her to say the answer. Slowly ask the questions listed below. Repeat each question as necessary. If your child's answer is not clear, ask "What do you mean?" or "Can you tell me more about that?"

Question	Answers
1. Why do people wash their hands?	To keep them clean.
2. Why should people eat fruit?	Fruit keeps you healthy.
3. Why do cars have airbags?	To prevent injuries in a car accident.
4. What should you do if you see people stealing from a store?	Call the police.
5. What should you do if you see a small child wandering around by himself?	Ask an adult to look for the parents.
6. What should you do if your house catches fire?	Call 911.
7. What should you do if you find someone's keys on the school playground?	Turn them in to a teacher or administrator.
8. Why do people need watches?	To know the time; To make sure they are punctual.
9. Why should we recycle and save water?	To conserve energy, reduce pollution and save money.
10. Why do some teachers not allow students to bring toys to class?	Toys are a distraction and students need to pay attention in order to learn.
11. Why should children clean their rooms?	To learn independence and responsibility.
12. Why do drivers need to obey speed limits?	To avoid accidents.
13. What are the advantages of reading books versus watching TV?	Books give more detail and can be taken anywhere.
14. Why are elections important in a democracy?	So that everyone's voice is heard.
15. Why should you keep your word?	So that people will trust you.
16. Why do adults pay taxes?	To pay for schools, roads, etc.

Question	Answers
17. Why is it bad to "show off" when you win a game?	It may make other people feel bad about themselves.
18. Why do teachers need to be certified to teach?	To make sure they are qualified and keep current on new educational practices.
19. What are the advantages of having public schools?	All children have access to education whether that have money or not.
20. What does this saying mean? "Education is not the filling of a vessel but the lighting of a fire."	Learning is not about filling your mind with facts and data, but about igniting a student's interests and passions.
21. Why should people exercise regularly?	To stay healthy and strong.
22. Why is it good to admit fault when you make a mistake?	So that people know that you are sorry.
23. Why do students sometimes plant gardens, conduct science experiments, and go to museums?	Because experiences can teach information you can't learn in a classroom.
24. Why should you not play loud music late at night?	To be considerate of your neighbors.
25. Why do soldiers wear uniforms?	To demonstrate authority.
26. If someone picks a fight with you, what should you do?	Walk away; do not fight.
27. If you accidentally break something that belongs to someone else, what should you do?	Admit fault and apologize.
28. Why is it bad to lie?	People will not trust you.
29. What does this saying mean? "Don't spend time beating on a wall hoping to transform it into a door."	Don't continue to do the same thing repeatedly expecting a different result. Try a new approach to achieve your goals.
30. What should you do if you see that your neighbor has fallen and been badly hurt?	Call 911.
31. What does this saying mean? "A smooth sea never made a skillful mariner."	Stress can help motivate you to work harder, better and succeed.
32. Why is it bad for athletes to use drugs to enhance their performance?	It's unfair to the athletes who succeed through hard work.
33. What are some problems with the increased use of social media?	Poor face-to-face social skills, spread of false information, cyberbullying, lower grades
34. What does this saying mean? "As you sow, so shall you reap."	If you do good things, good things will happen to you. If you do bad things, bad things will happen to you.

Description
During the similarities subtest, the examiner asks the child to explain how two similar objects or concepts are similar.

Instructions
Read the sentences to your child. If the answer is not clear, ask "What do you mean?" or "Can you tell me more about that?" Begin by saying: **"Now I'm going to ask you a few questions about how things are alike. Let's start with..."**

1. How are a crayon and pencil alike? (things you write with)

2. How are orange juice and soda alike? (liquids; drinks)

3. How are a peach and a pear alike? (fruit)

4. How are a coat and a boot alike? (clothing)

5. How are a fly and a ladybug alike? (bugs; insects)

6. How are a pig and a goat alike? (animals)

7. How are pennies and nickels alike? (coins; money)

8. How are father and daughter alike? (family)

9. How are fall and spring alike? (seasons)

10. How are fear and sadness alike? (emotions)

11. How are a car and a plane alike? (vehicles; thing to travel in)

12. How are magazines and newspapers alike? (reading materials)

13. How are a restaurant and a grocery store alike? (places you can get food)

14. How are a house and an apartment alike? (places people live)

15. How are ice cream and snow alike? (cold)

16. How are bricks and cement alike? (building materials; used to make things)

17. How are cold and hot alike? (temperatures)

18. How are a scale and a ruler alike? (tools for measurement)

19. How are G and K alike? (letters)

20. How are 9 and 5 alike? (numbers)

21. How are blue and yellow alike? (colors)

22. How are breakfast and dinner alike? (meals)

23. How are tennis and baseball alike? (sports)

24. How are eyes and mouth alike? (parts of the face/5 senses)

25. How are rain and wind alike? (weather)

26. How are glue and nails alike? (they hold things together)

27. How are vapor and hail alike? (phases of water)

28. How are sweet and bitter alike? (tastes)

29. How are a bed and a sofa alike? (furniture)

30. How are a rose and a tulip alike? (flowers)

31. How are taste and touch alike? (senses)

32. How are morning and evening alike? (times of day)

33. How are pots and pans alike? (used for cooking)

34. How are cookies and cake alike? (sweets)

35. How are a lake and a volcano alike? (geographical elements)

36. How are a bedroom and kitchen alike? (rooms in a house)

37. How are pretty and ugly alike? (descriptions of appearance)

38. How are command and implore alike? (ways to get someone to do something or help you)

39. How are a finger and an elbow alike? (joints)

40. How are a grin and a frown alike? (facial expressions)

41. How are heat and electricity alike? (types of kinetic energy)

42. How are preparation and planning alike? (things that influence success)

43. How are a photographer and a writer alike? (artists)

44. How are beginning and end alike? (part of a sequence)

45. How are a hurricane and earthquake alike? (forces of nature)

46. How are a reflection and a footprint alike? (reproductions; duplications)

47. How are oxygen and water alike? (people need them to live)

48. How are retaliation and mercy alike? (choices you can make if someone hurts you)

49. How are consent and restriction alike? (ways to control)

50. How are alert and drowsy alike? (states of mind)

51. How are Confucius and Socrates alike? (famous philosophers)

Block Design

Description
During the block design subtest, your child will be asked to arrange blocks according to a specific model or picture under time-constraints. Your child must complete each block design correctly within the time limit. The maximum points will be received for designs that are constructed correctly (without rotation errors) within the time limit on the first trial.

Materials
• 9 blue and white blocks (must be purchased separately)
• Clock or stopwatch

Instructions
Seat your child at a table directly facing you. Designs 1 and 2 are models that should be built in front of your child. Designs 3-40 are pictures. For Design 3, show your child the picture, then build the design in front of him. For Designs 4-40, show the picture to your child, but do not build the designs. Begin timing for each design after saying the instructions. Stop timing when your child has completed the design. Rotated designs are considered incorrect. Be sure to correct any rotated design constructions. During the exercise administration, if your child answers more than 3 questions in a row incorrectly, he/she may need a brief rest or may need to move on to a new activity.

Design 1 (Time Limit: 30 sec.)

Place 3 blocks in front of your child and show him that some sides are all blue, some sides are all white and some sides are blue and white. Then say: **"Let's play a game with these blocks. First, I'm going to build something with the blocks, then I want you to copy it."**

Build the first design in front of your child. Then, give your child his/her own set of 3 blocks and say: **"Now I want you to make this as fast as you can. Are you ready. Go ahead."** Begin timing. Stop when the design is completed. Write the completion time in the space below. If the design is completed successfully, move on to the next design. If not, build the design again using your child's blocks. Then ask him to try again once more.

Time: _____ seconds.

Design 2 (Time Limit: 45 sec.)

Place 4 blocks in front of your child and say: **"Let's try another one. Watch this."**

Build Design 2 in front of your child. Then, give your child his/her own set of 4 blocks and say: **"Now it's your turn to make it as fast as you can. Get ready. Go."** Begin timing. Stop when the design is completed. Write the completion time in the space below. If the design is completed successfully, move on to the next design. If not, build the design again using your child's blocks. Then ask him to try again once more.

Time: _____ seconds.

Design 3 (Time Limit: 45 sec.)

Place 4 blocks in front of your child, with only 1 two-color side facing up. Turn to Design 3 on page 41. Then say: **"Look at this picture. I'm going to make this picture with the blocks. Watch me."**

Build Design 3 in front of the child. Then, disassemble the block design. Give the blocks, with 1 two-color side facing up, to your child. Then say: **"Now you give it a try. Go as fast as you can. Are you ready? Go."**

Begin timing. Stop when the design is completed. Write the completion time in the space below. If the child builds the design incorrectly, ask him to try once more.

Time: _____ seconds.

Designs 4-12 (Time Limit: Designs 4-7: 45 sec./Designs 8-12: 75 sec.)

Place 4 blocks in front of your child with 1 two-color side facing up. Turn to the appropriate design and say: **"Now it's your turn to make these blocks look like this picture. Go as fast as you can. Get ready. Go."** Begin timing. Stop when the design is completed. Write the completion time in the space provided.

Designs 13-40 (Time Limit: 120 sec.)

Place 9 blocks in front of your child with 2 two-color sides facing up. Turn to the appropriate design and say: **"Now it's your turn to make these blocks look like this picture. Go as fast as you can. Get ready. Go."** Begin timing. Stop when the design is completed. Write the completion time in the space provided.

3

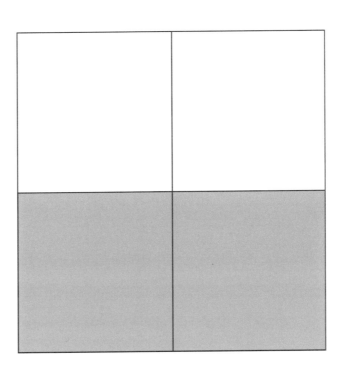

Time: _____ seconds (Max. 45 sec.)

4

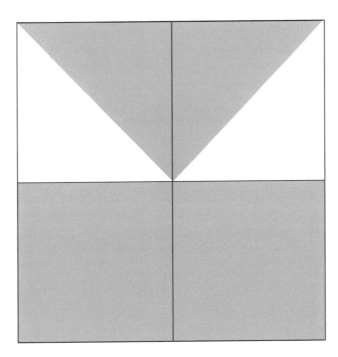

Time: _____ seconds (Max. 45 sec.)

5

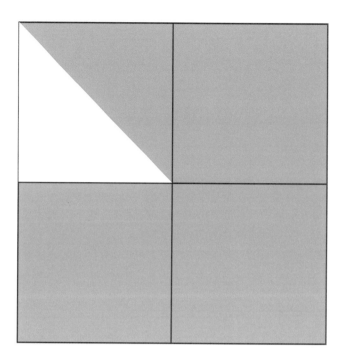

Time: _____ seconds (Max. 45 sec.)

6

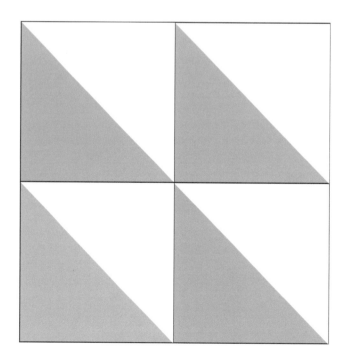

Time: _____ seconds (Max. 45 sec.)

7

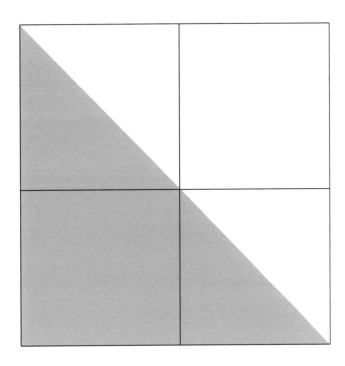

Time: _____ seconds (Max. 45 sec.)

8

Time: _____ seconds (Max. 75 sec.)

9

Time: _____ seconds (Max. 75 sec.)

10

Time: _____ seconds (Max. 75 sec.)

11

Time: _____ seconds (Max. 75 sec.)

12

Time: _____ seconds (Max. 75 sec.)

13

Time: _____ seconds (Max. 120 sec.)

14

Time: _____ seconds (Max. 120 sec.)

15

Time: _____ seconds (Max. 120 sec.)

16

Time: _____ seconds (Max. 120 sec.)

17

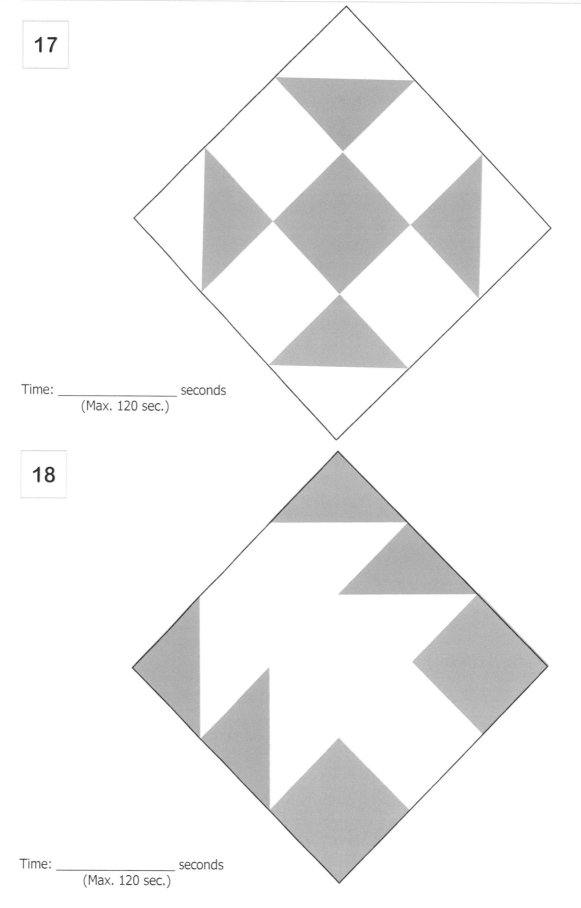

Time: _____ seconds
(Max. 120 sec.)

18

Time: _____ seconds
(Max. 120 sec.)

19

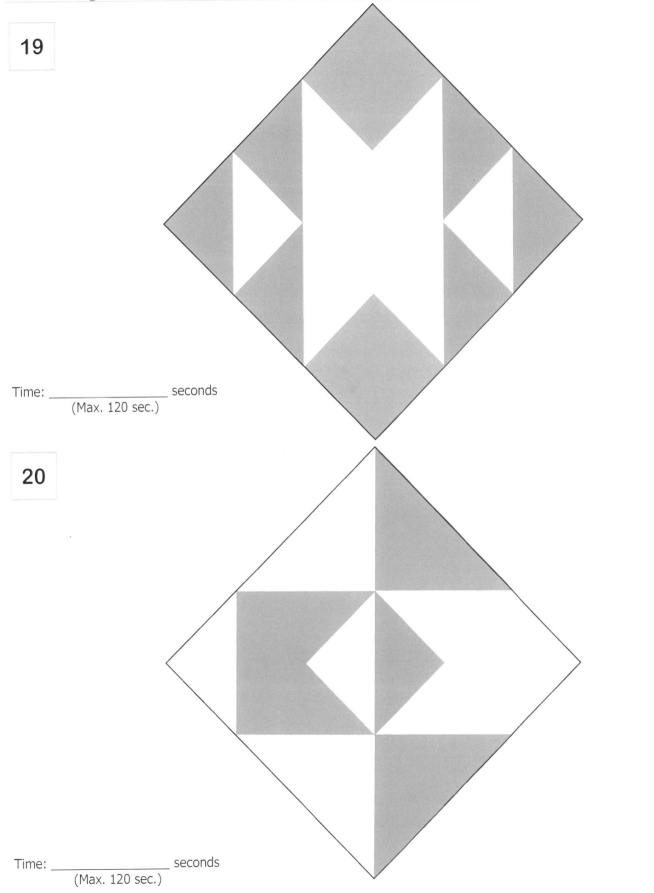

Time: _____ seconds
(Max. 120 sec.)

20

Time: _____ seconds
(Max. 120 sec.)

21

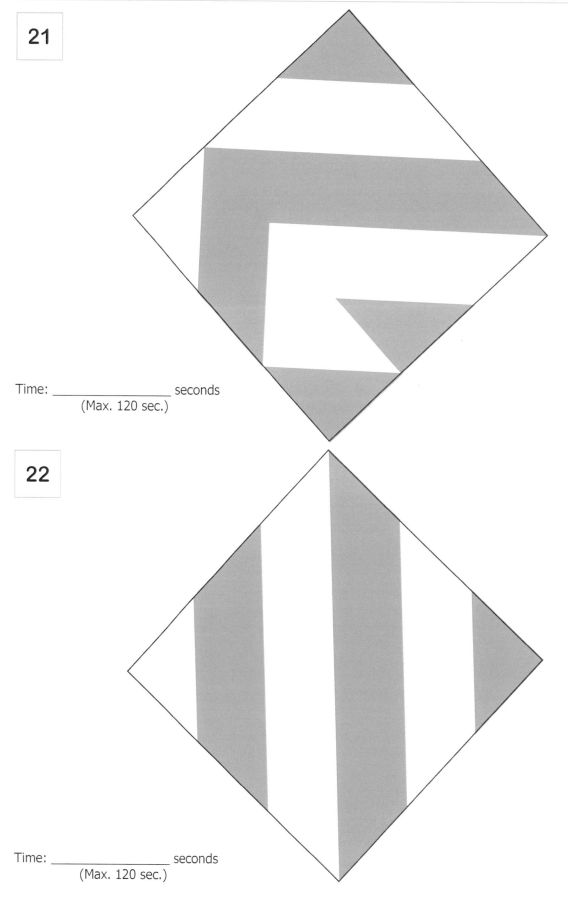

Time: _____ seconds
(Max. 120 sec.)

22

Time: _____ seconds
(Max. 120 sec.)

23

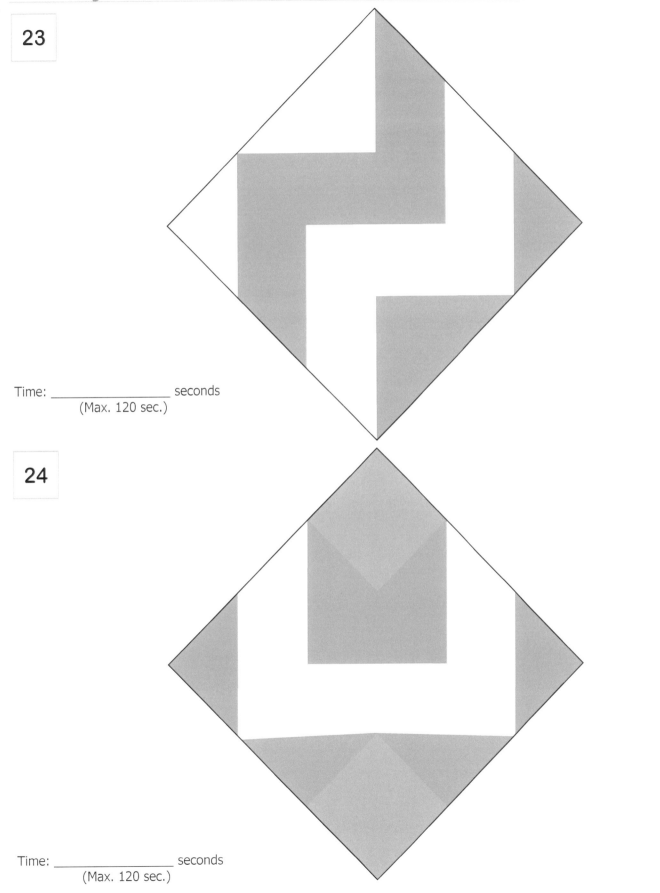

Time: _____ seconds
(Max. 120 sec.)

24

Time: _____ seconds
(Max. 120 sec.)

52

25

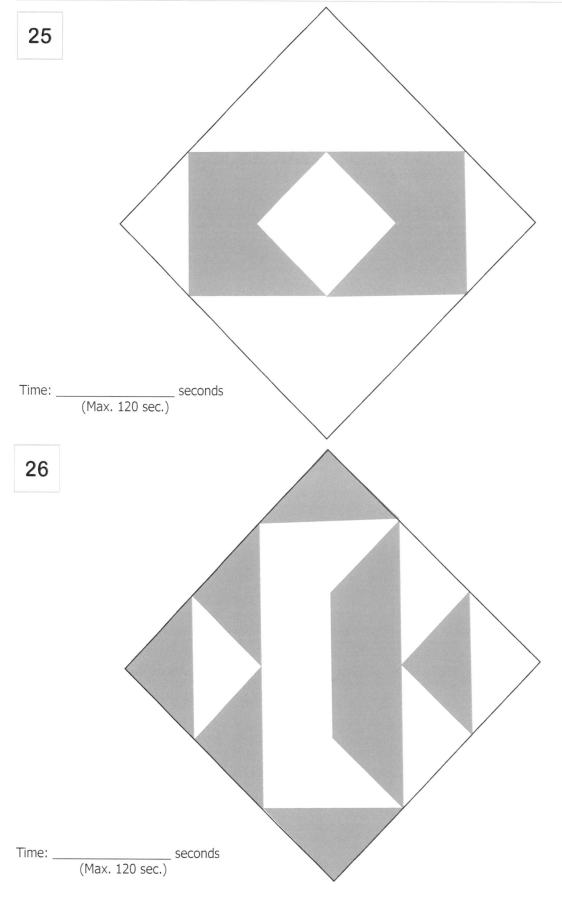

Time: _____ seconds
(Max. 120 sec.)

26

Time: _____ seconds
(Max. 120 sec.)

Block Design

27

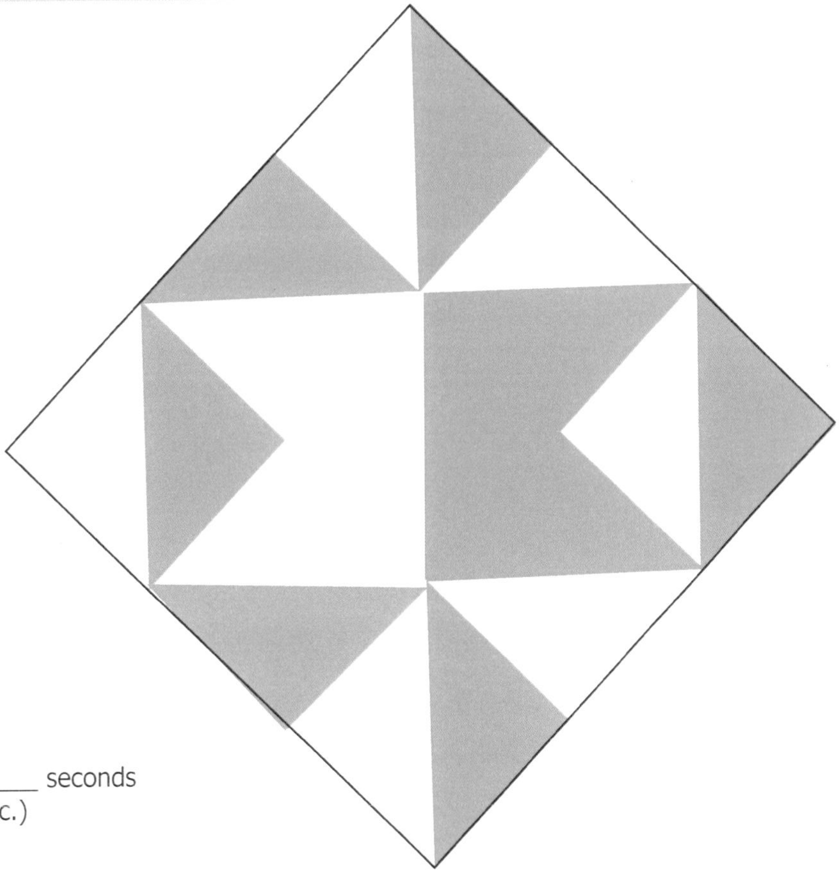

Time: _____ seconds
(Max. 120 sec.)

28

Time: _____ seconds
(Max. 120 sec.)

29

Time: _____ seconds
(Max. 120 sec.)

30

Time: _____ seconds
(Max. 120 sec.)

31

Time: _____ seconds
(Max. 120 sec.)

32

Time: _____ seconds
(Max. 120 sec.)

33

Time: _____ seconds
(Max. 120 sec.)

34

Time: _____ seconds
(Max. 120 sec.)

35

Time: _____ seconds
(Max. 120 sec.)

36

Time: _____ seconds
(Max. 120 sec.)

37

Time: _____ seconds
(Max. 120 sec.)

38

Time: _____ seconds
(Max. 120 sec.)

39

Time: _____ seconds
(Max. 120 sec.)

40

Time: _____ seconds
(Max. 120 sec.)

Description

During the visual puzzles subtest, your child will view a completed puzzle and within 30 seconds must choose the three response items that would combine to reconstruct the puzzle. Some of the more difficult puzzles will include pieces that will only fit the puzzle if they are rotated.

Instructions

Children of all ages should begin with exercise one. Place the first visual puzzle in front of your child and say:

"Look at this shape; (point to the green circle) **it is a completed puzzle. Three of these shapes** (point to the answer choices in the numbered boxes) **go together to make this puzzle** (point to the green circle). **Which shapes go together to make this puzzle?"**

Your child must answer within 30 seconds. He must either point to the answer or say the number of the answer. If he misses 3 or 4 in a row, he may need to take a break and return to it later. Check his responses on page 87. For any incorrect responses, review the answer explanations and carefully explain how the answer choices complete the puzzle.

1

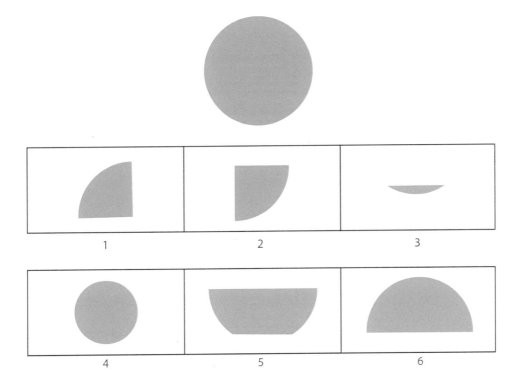

2

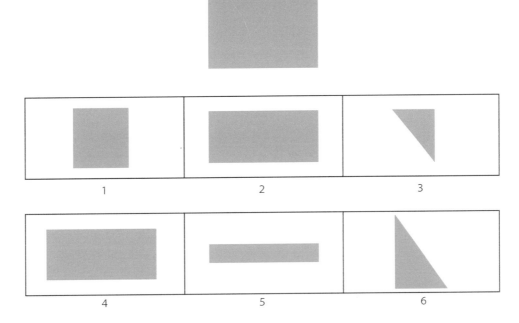

3

1 2 3

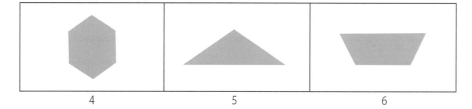

4 5 6

4

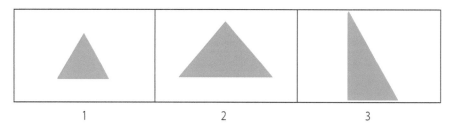

1 2 3

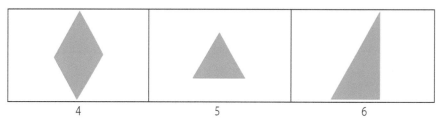

4 5 6

5

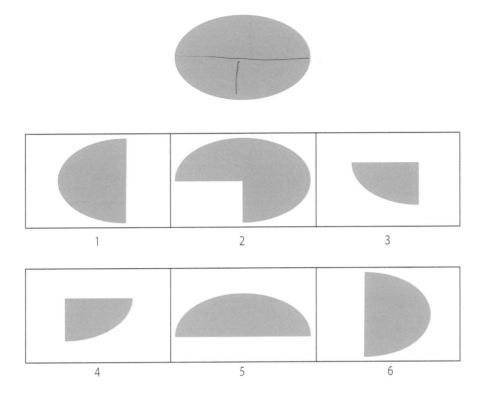

6

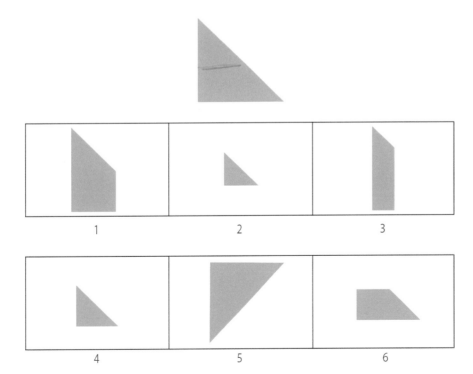

7

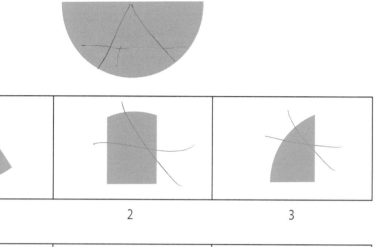

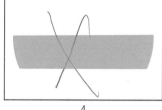		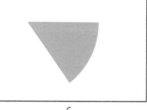
1	2	3

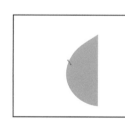	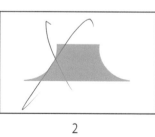	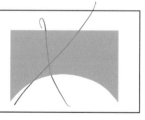
4	5	6

8

1	2	3

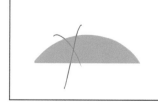		
4	5	6

9

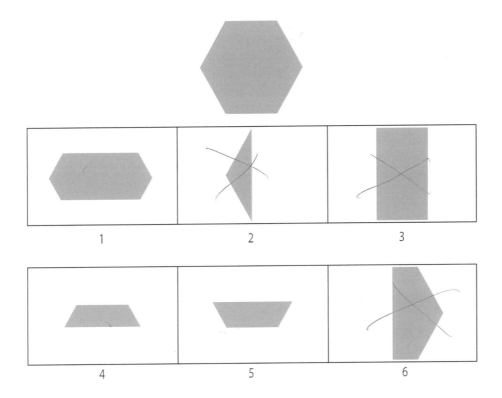

10

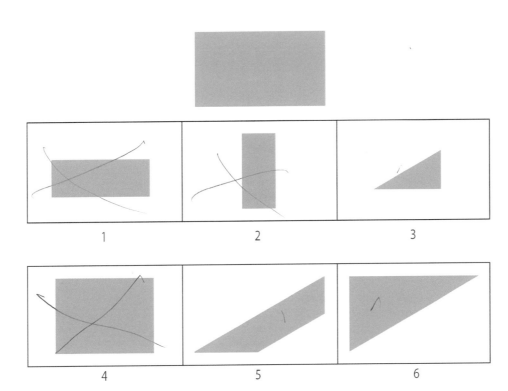

11

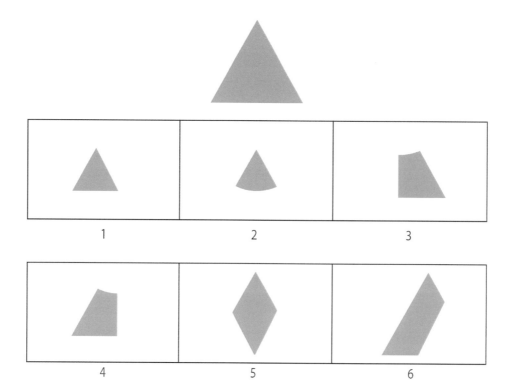

12

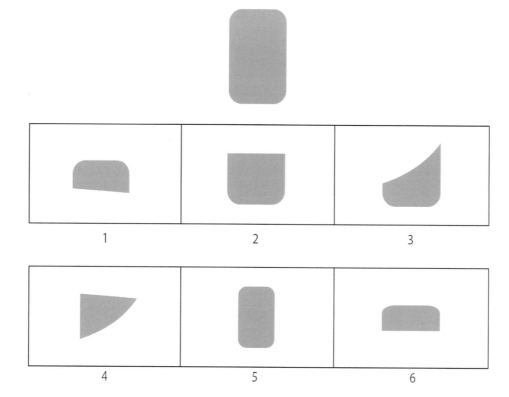

13

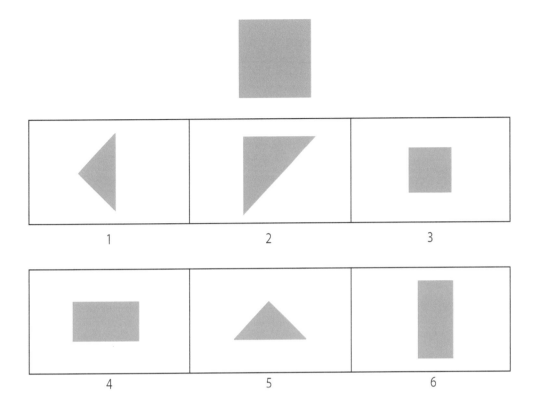

14

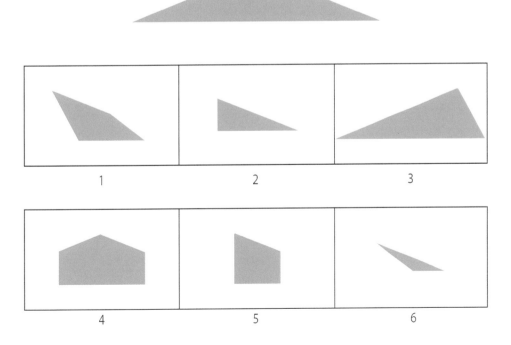

15

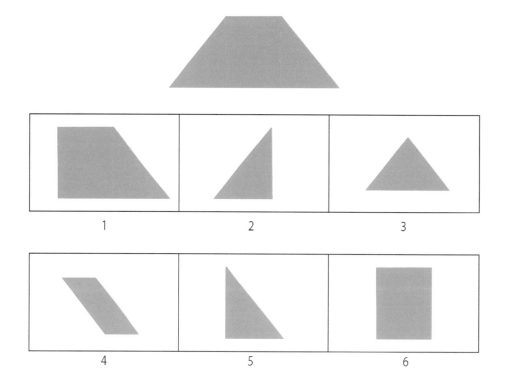

16

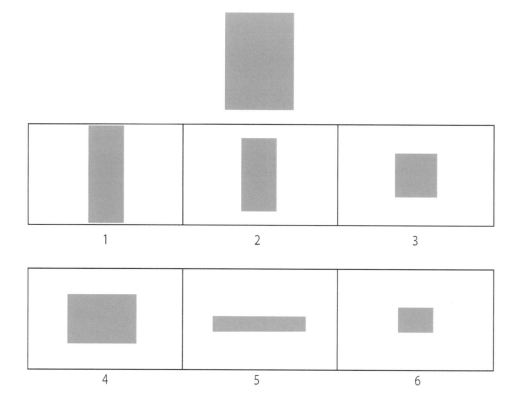

17

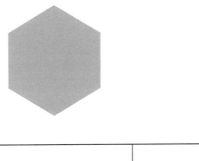

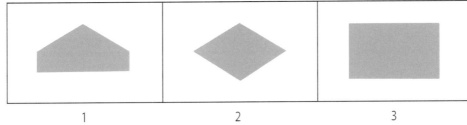

1   2   3

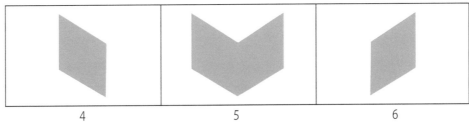

4   5   6

18

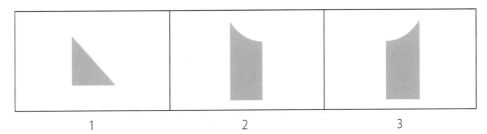

1   2   3

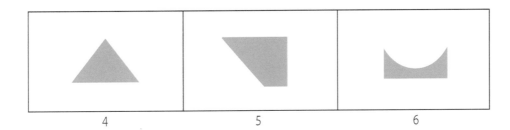

4   5   6

19

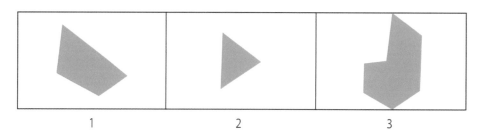

1   2   3

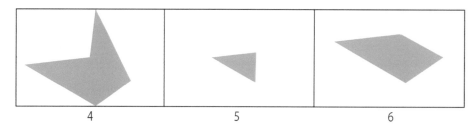

4   5   6

20

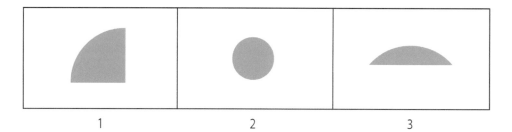

1   2   3

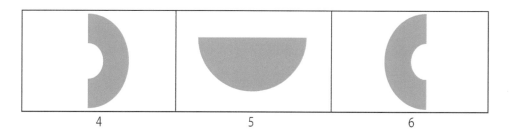

4   5   6

21

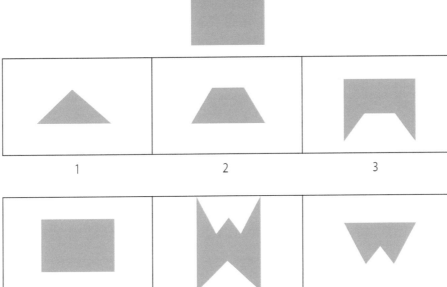

1	2	3

4	5	6

22

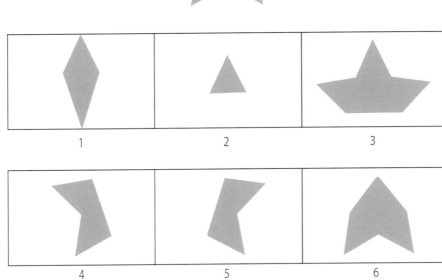

1	2	3

4	5	6

23

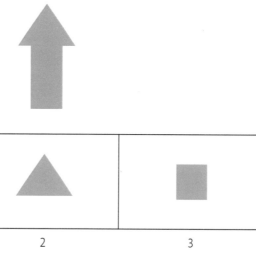

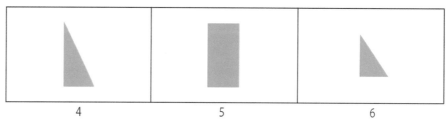

| 1 | 2 | 3 |

| 4 | 5 | 6 |

24

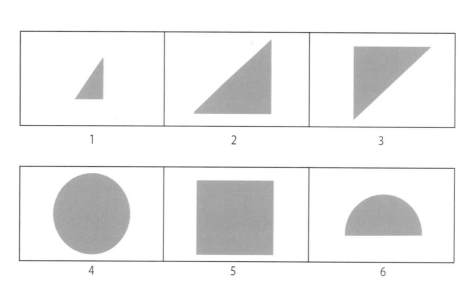

| 1 | 2 | 3 |

| 4 | 5 | 6 |

25

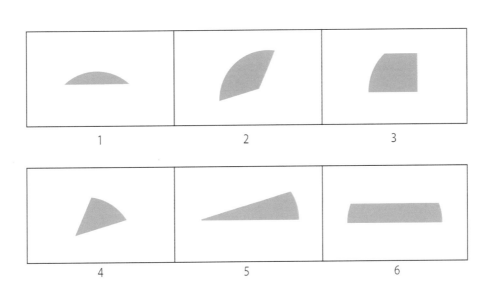

26

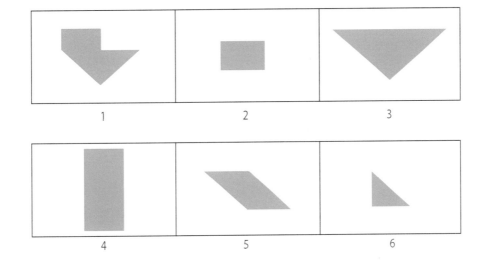

27

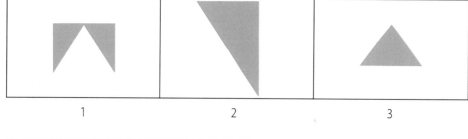

1   2   3

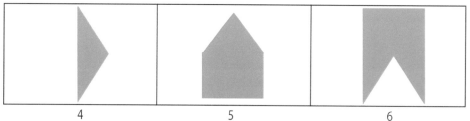

4   5   6

28

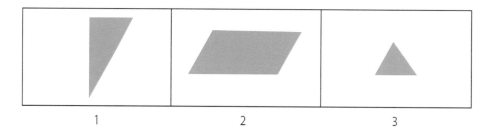

1   2   3

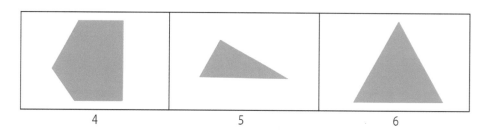

4   5   6

29

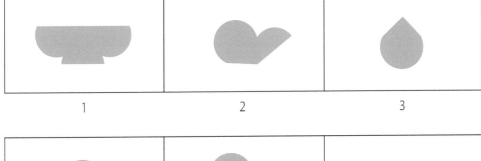

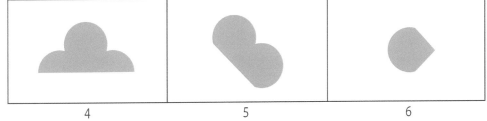

30

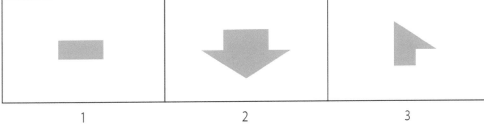

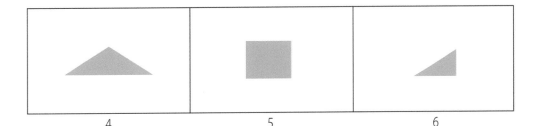

31

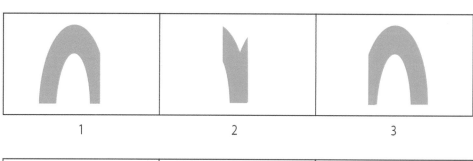

1	2	3

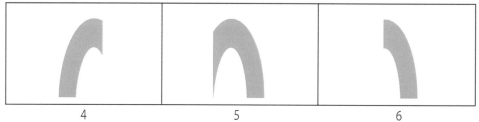

4	5	6

32

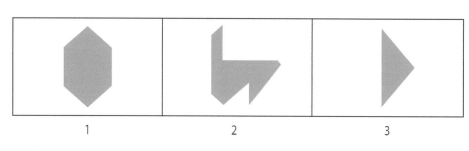

1	2	3

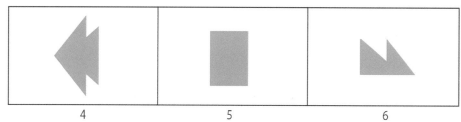

4	5	6

33

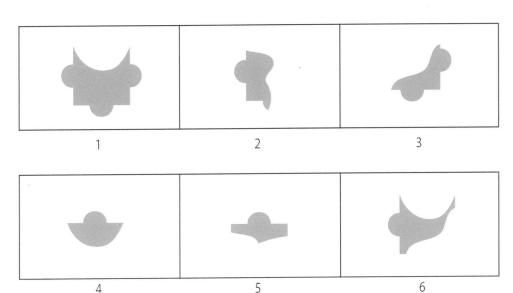

1 2 3

4 5 6

34

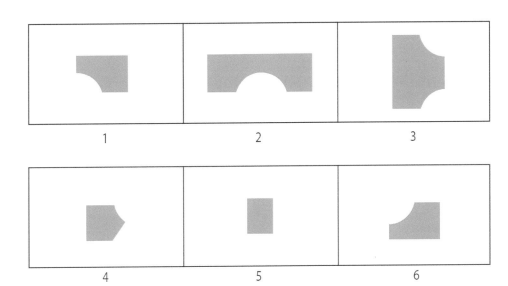

1 2 3

4 5 6

35

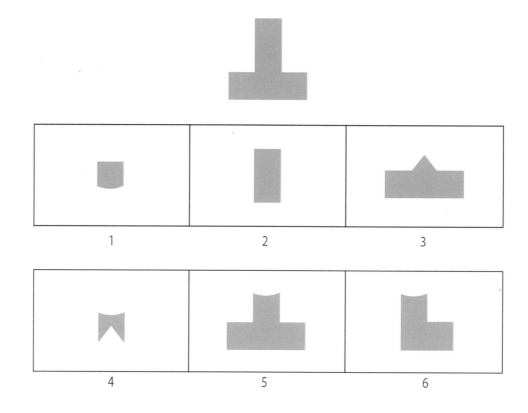

36

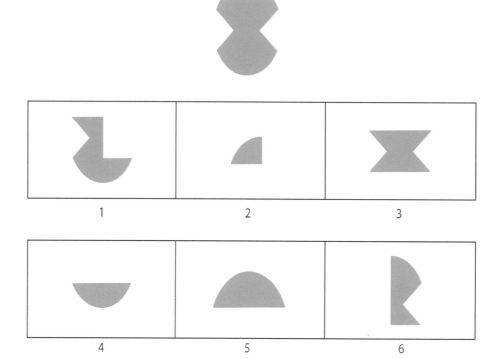

37

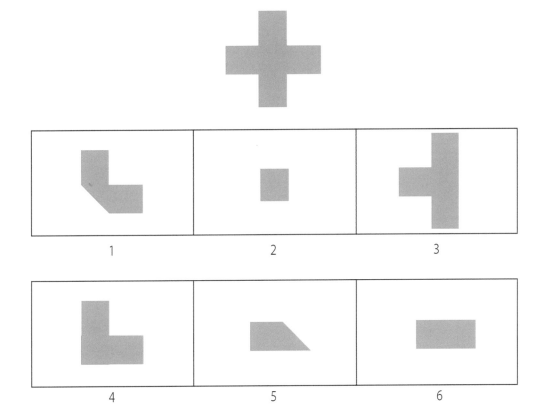

38

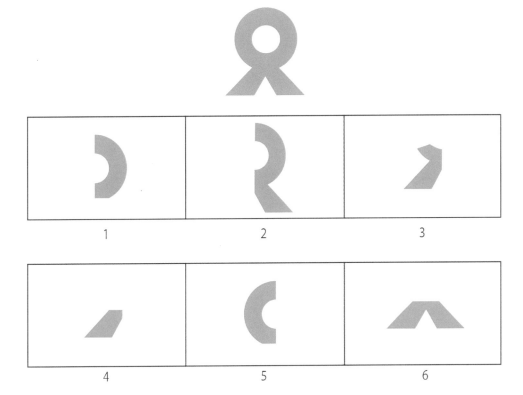

39

1   2   3

4   5   6

40

1   2   3

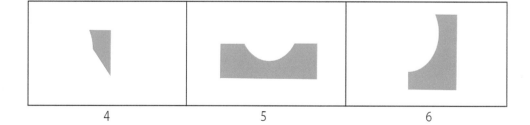

4   5   6

41

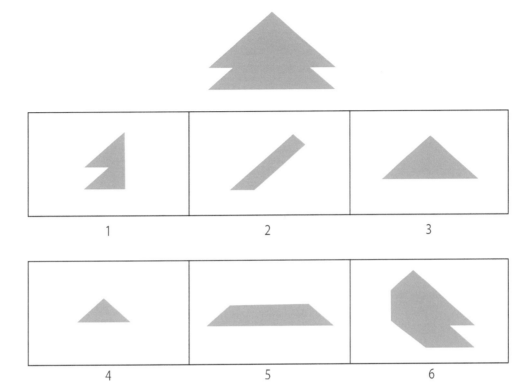

1

2

3

4

5

6

42

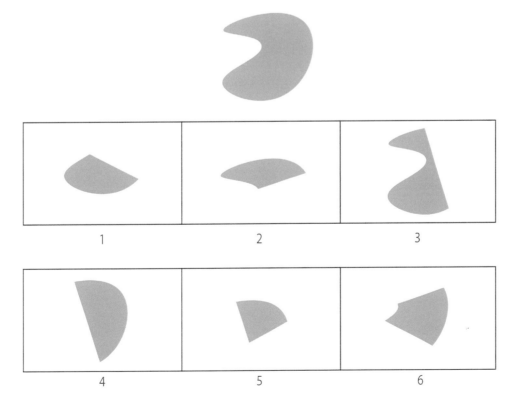

1

2

3

4

5

6

43

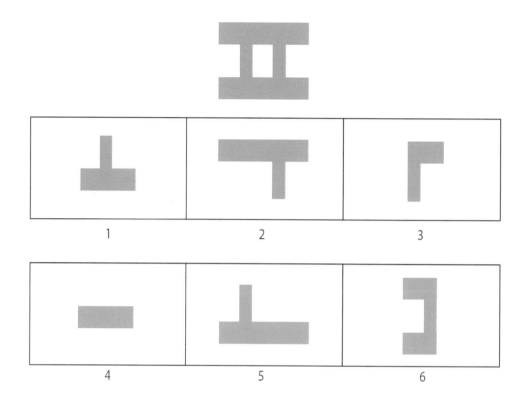

44

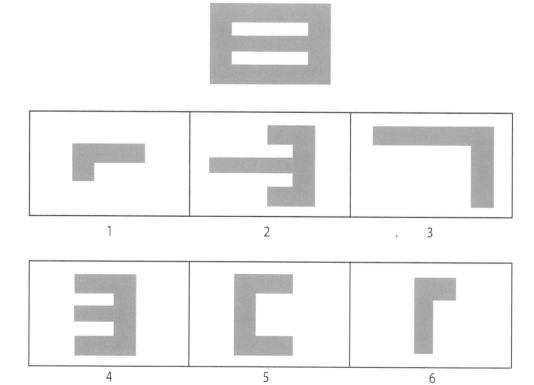

45

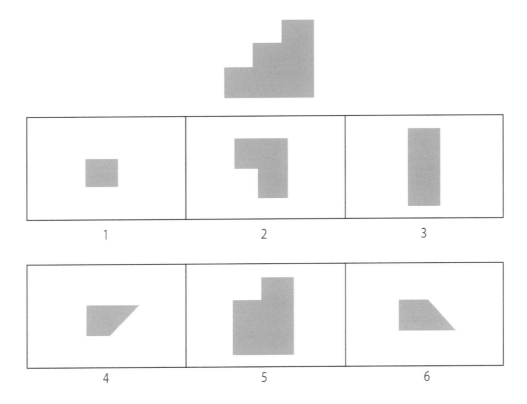

46

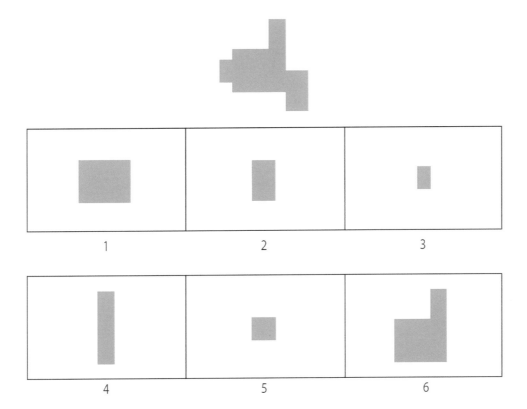

47

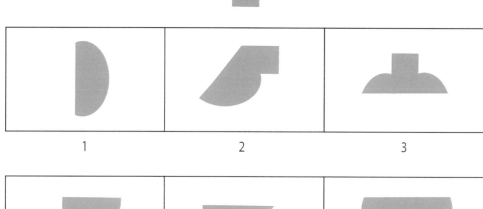

1 2 3

4 5 6

48

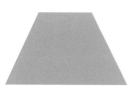

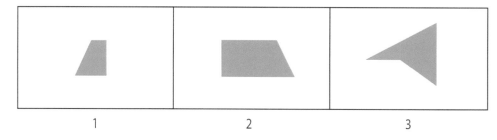

1 2 3

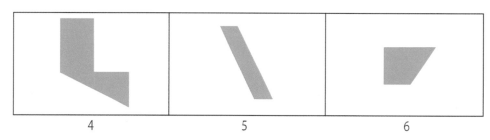

4 5 6

49

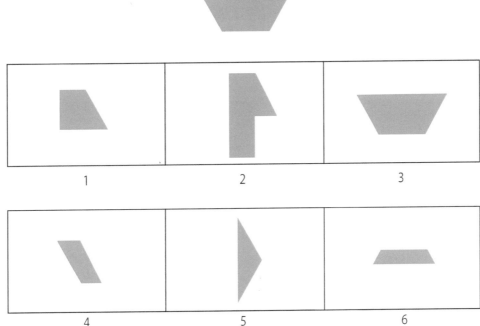

50

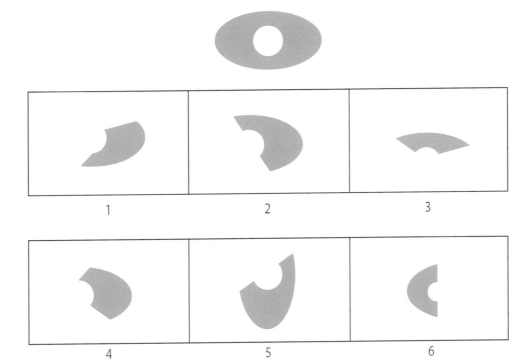

51

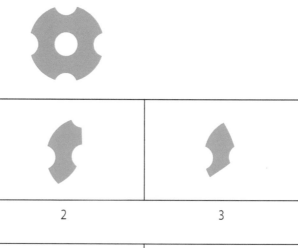

| 1 | 2 | 3 |

| 4 | 5 | 6 |

52

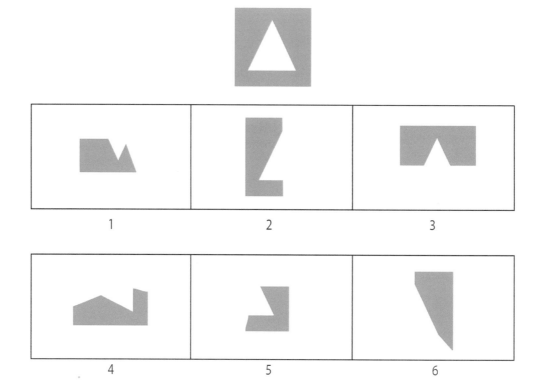

| 1 | 2 | 3 |

| 4 | 5 | 6 |

Answer Key

1. 3, 5, 6

2. 2, 4, 5

3. 1, 2, 5

4. 1, 4, 5

5. 3, 4, 5

6. 2, 3, 6

7. 1, 5, 6

8. 1, 5, 6

9. 1, 4, 5

10. 3, 5, 6

11. 2, 3, 4

12. 1, 3, 4

13. 1, 2, 5

14. 1, 3, 6

15. 2, 5, 6

16. 1, 2, 6

17. 2, 4, 6

18. 1, 5, 6

19. 2, 3, 5

20. 2, 4, 6

21. 1, 5, 6

22. 1, 4, 5

23. 1, 5, 6

24. 2, 3, 6

25. 2, 4, 5

26. 1, 2, 5

27. 2, 3, 4

28. 1, 3, 4

29. 3, 5, 6

30. 1, 2, 4

31. 2, 4, 5

32. 2, 4, 6

33. 3, 4, 6

34. 1, 3, 6

35. 1, 3, 4

36. 1, 2, 6

37. 1, 2, 5

38. 2, 4, 5

39. 1, 3, 5

40. 2, 3, 4

41. 2, 3, 5

42. 1, 2, 6

43. 1, 4, 6

44. 1, 2, 6 (rotated 90 degrees)

45. 3, 4 (rotated 90 degrees), 6

46. 2, 3, 6

47. 1, 2 (rotated 90 degrees), 5 (rotated 90 degrees)

48. 3 (rotated 90 degrees), 4 (rotated 90 degrees), 6

49. 2 (rotated 180 degrees), 4, 5

50. 1, 3, 4 (rotated 180 degrees)

51. 2, 5, 6

52. 1 (rotated 180 degrees), 4 (rotated 90 degrees), 5

Description

During the matrix reasoning subtest, your child must choose the correct response to complete the matrix. The items represent both real items and abstract designs.

Instructions

Turn to the matrix reasoning exercises on the next page. Place the exercises in front of your child and say:

"**Let's play a game. Look at this group of objects** (point to square matrix) **and tell me which one here** (point to bottom pictures) **goes here** (point to blank square)."

Your child must either point to the answer or say the number of the answer. If the answer is incorrect, explain why the correct answer completes the matrix. The answer key can be found on page 115.

1

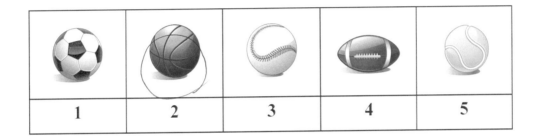

2

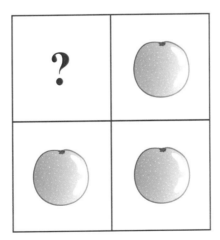

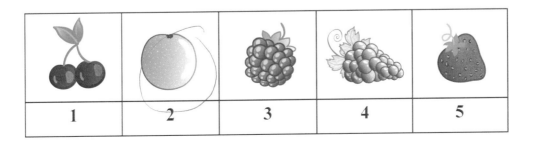

3

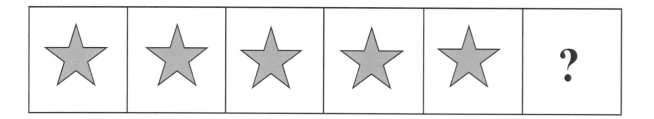

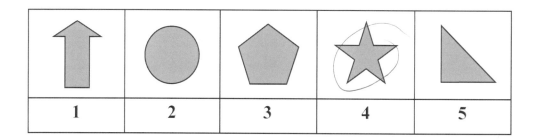

4

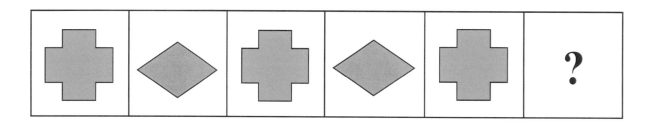

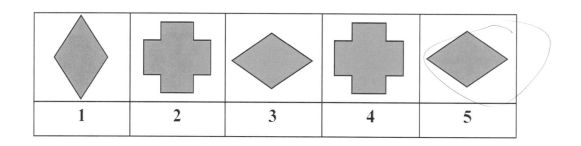

5

1	2	3	4	5

6

1	2	3	4	5

7

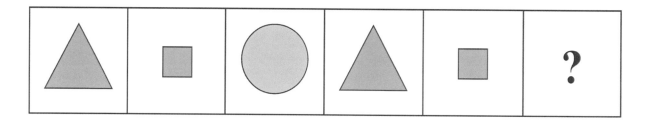

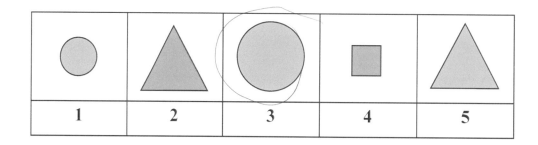

8

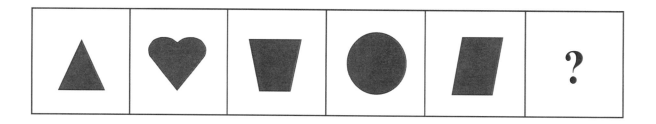

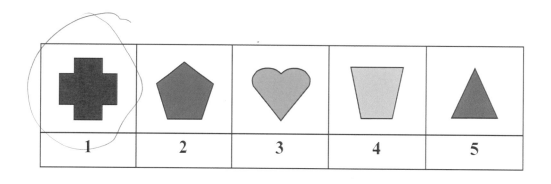

9

10

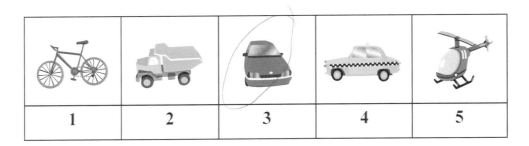

11

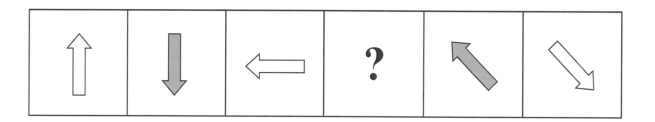

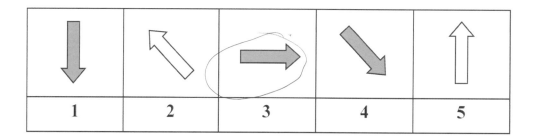

12

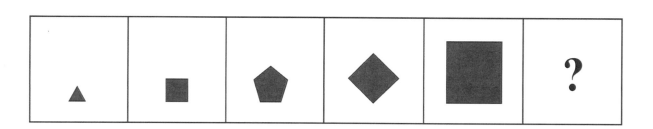

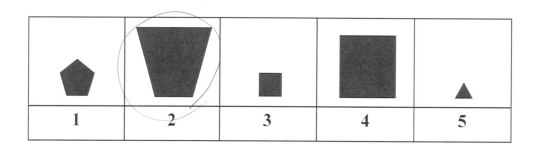

13

1	2	3	4	5

14

1	2	3	4	5

15

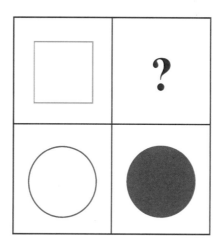

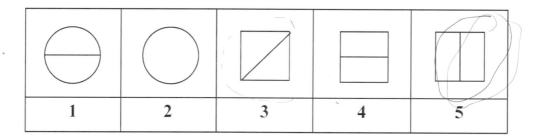

16

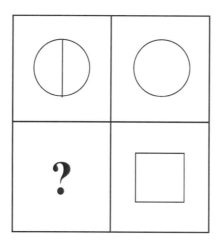

17

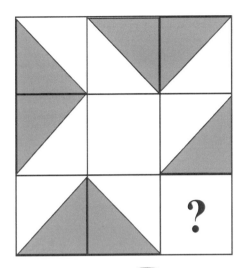

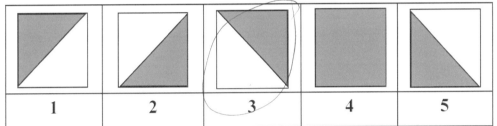

18

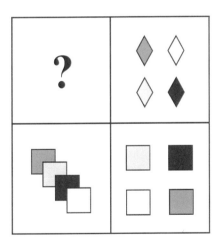

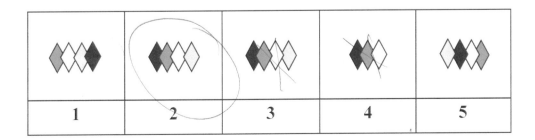

19

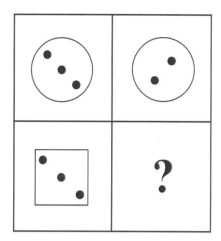

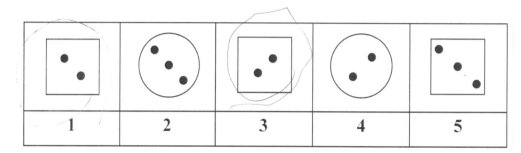

20

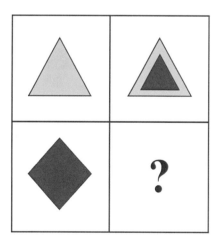

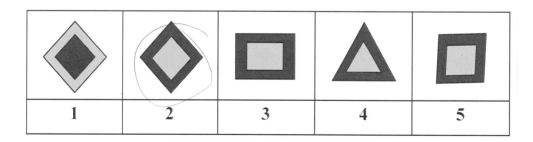

21

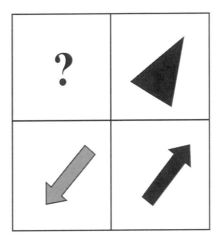

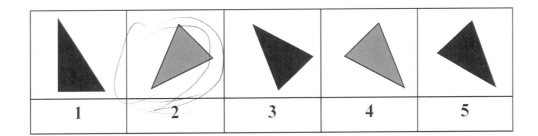

22

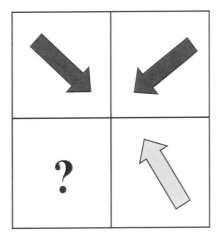

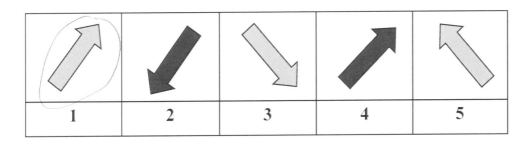

23

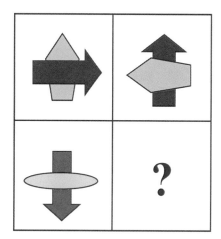

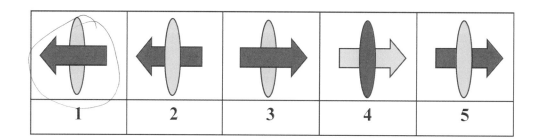

1	2	3	4	5

24

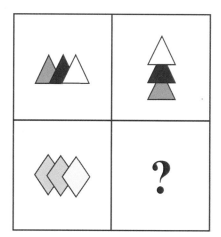

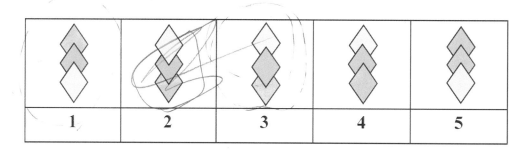

1	2	3	4	5

25

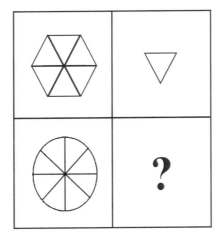

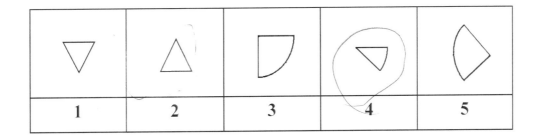

26

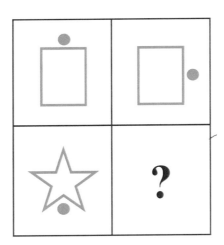

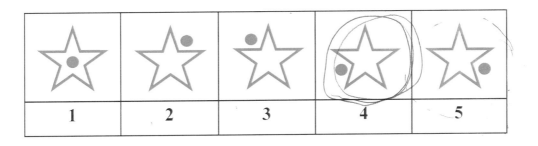

27

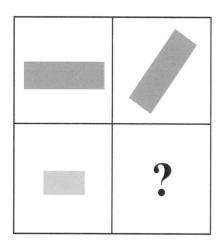

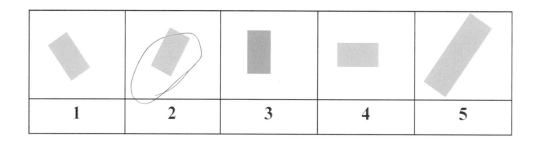

1	2	3	4	5

28

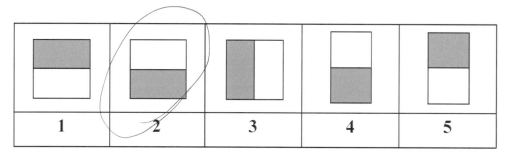

1	2	3	4	5

29

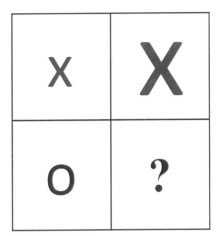

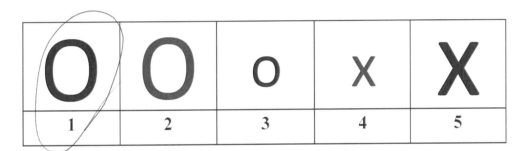

30

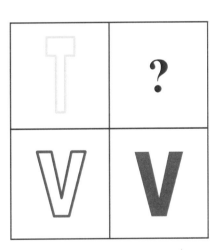

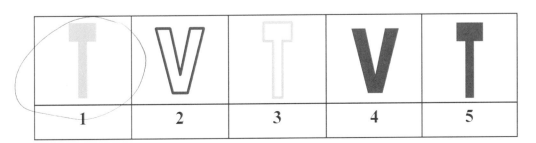

31

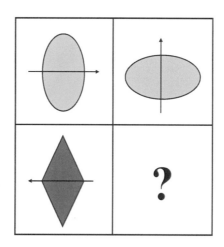

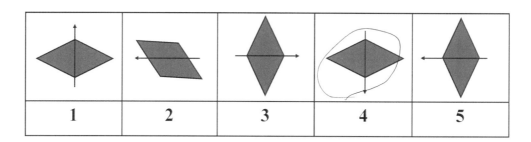

| 1 | 2 | 3 | 4 | 5 |

32

| 1 | 2 | 3 | 4 | 5 |

33

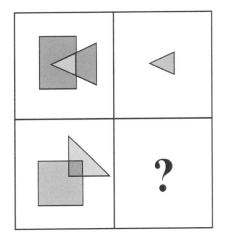

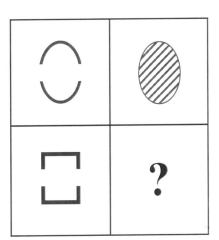

34

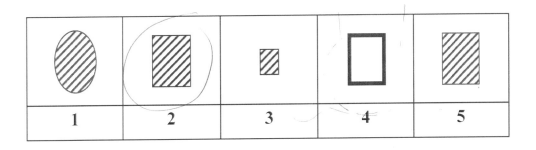

35

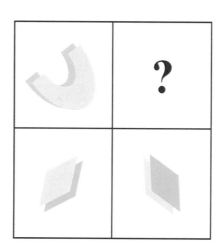

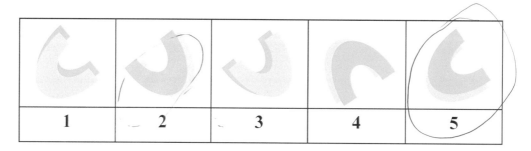

1	2	3	4	5

36

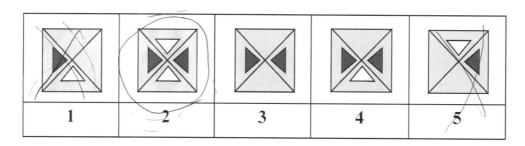

1	2	3	4	5

37

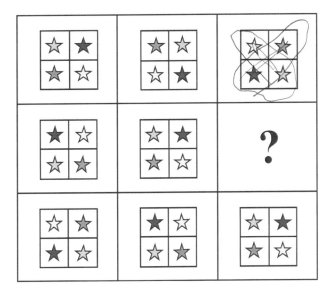

38

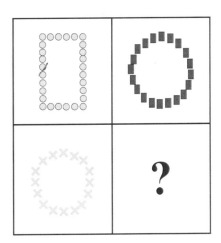

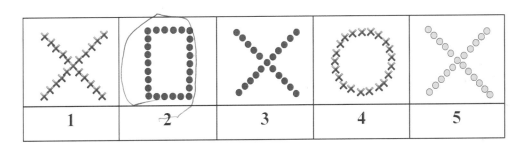

39

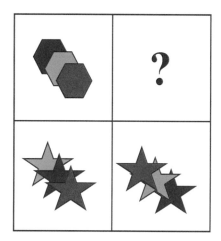

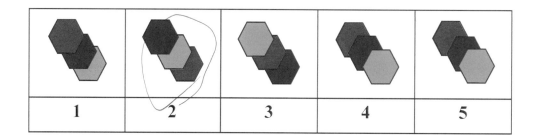

| 1 | 2 | 3 | 4 | 5 |

40

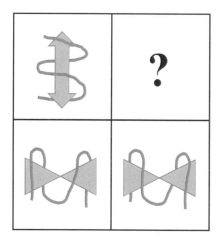

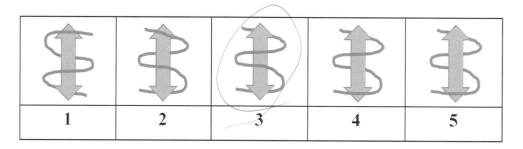

| 1 | 2 | 3 | 4 | 5 |

41

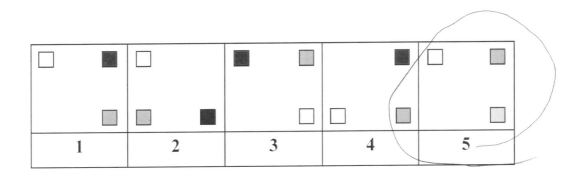

42

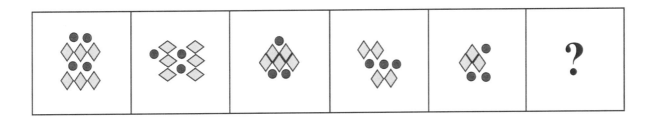

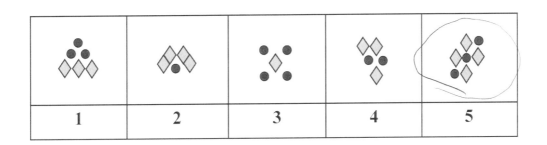

43

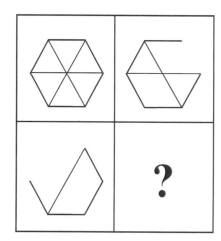

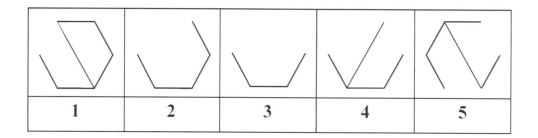

44

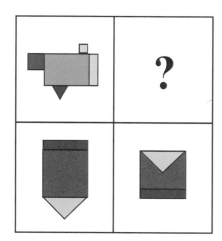

45

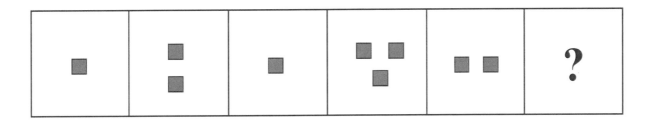

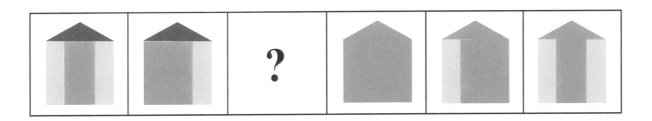

46

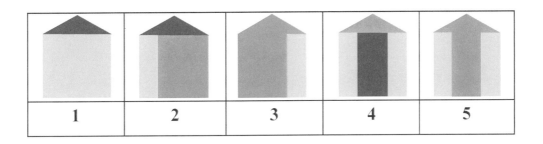

47

1	2	3	4	5

48

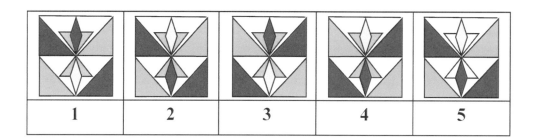

1	2	3	4	5

49

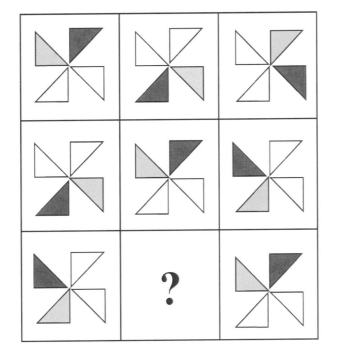

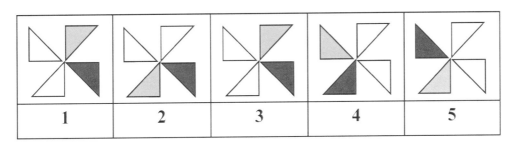

50

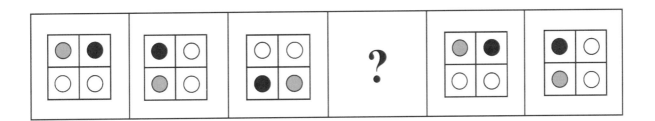

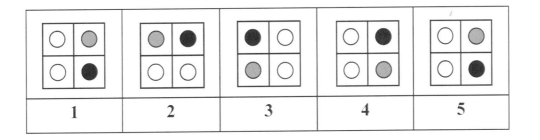

51

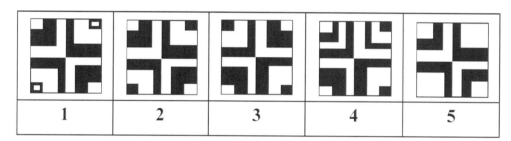

52

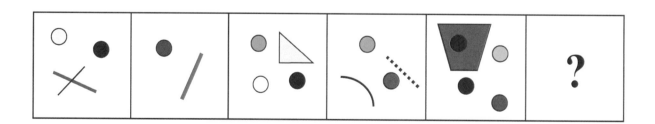

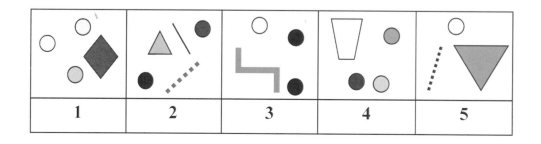

Matrix Reasoning

Matrix	Answer
1	2
2	2
3	4
4	5
5	4
6	4
7	3
8	1
9	5
10	3
11	3
12	2
13	1
14	4
15	4
16	5
17	3
18	2
19	3
20	2
21	2
22	1
23	1
24	2
25	4
26	4
27	2

Matrix	Answer
28	2
29	1
30	1
31	4
32	2
33	3
34	2
35	5
36	5
37	2
38	3
39	1
40	4
41	1
42	4
43	3
44	5
45	5
46	3
47	2
48	2
49	1
50	5
51	2
52	3

Description

Your child will be shown 2 or 3 sets of objects and must choose 2 or 3 items that go together. Correct items are related by a common function or category.

Instructions

Turn to the picture concepts section on the next page.

For pictures 1-16 say:

"Look at these pictures. Pick the one on the first row (point to the first row) **that goes with the one on the second row** (point to the second row)."

For pictures 17-30 say:

"Look at these pictures. Pick the one here (point to the first row) **that goes with the one here** (point to the second row), **and goes with the one here** (point to the third row)."

Your child may name the picture, point to the picture, or say the picture number. Try to get him/her to respond within 30 seconds. Check your child's answers with the answer key on page 139.

1

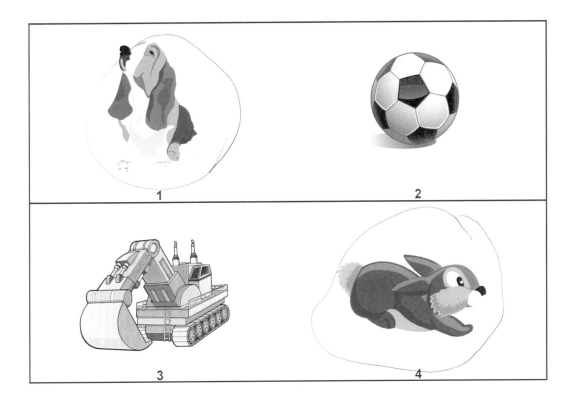

| 1 | 2 |
| 3 | 4 |

2

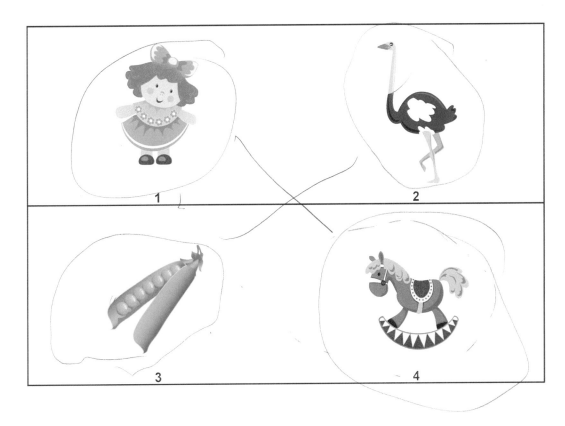

| 1 | 2 |
| 3 | 4 |

3

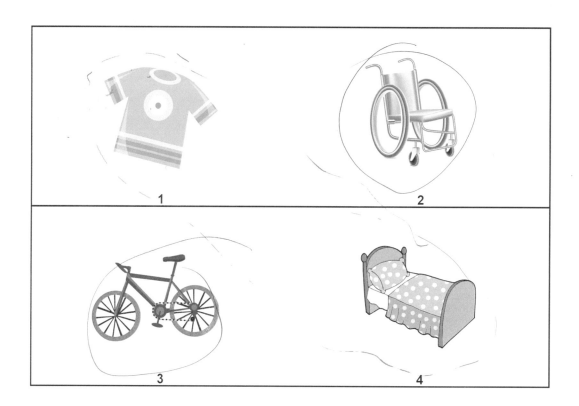

4

5

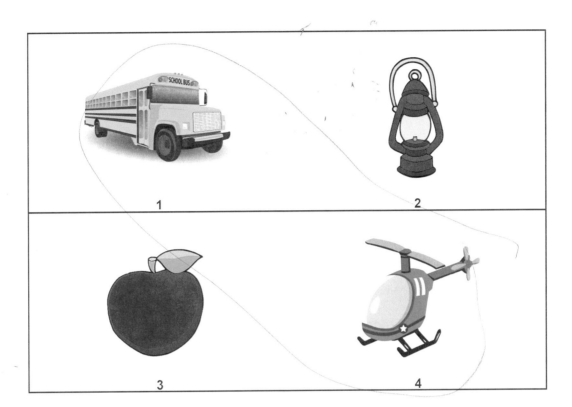

1

2

3

4

6

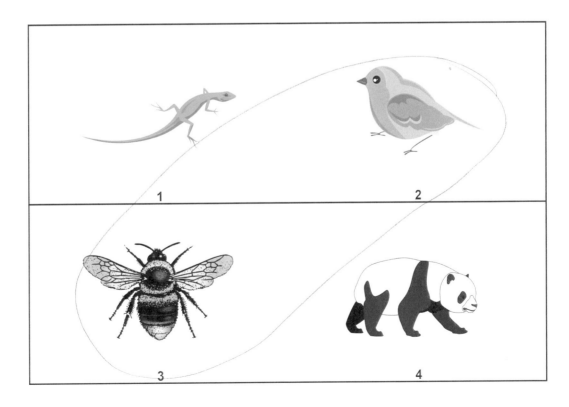

1

2

3

4

7

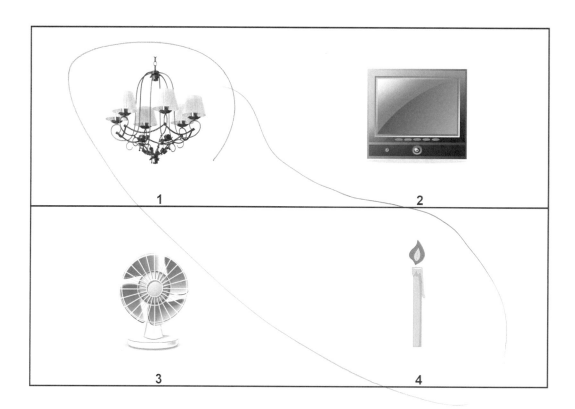

8

9

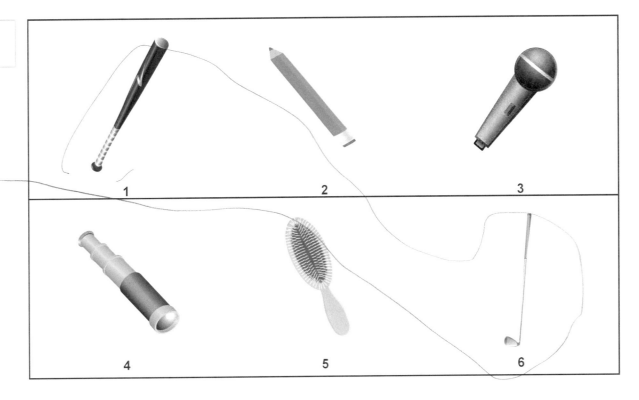

1   2   3

4   5   6

10

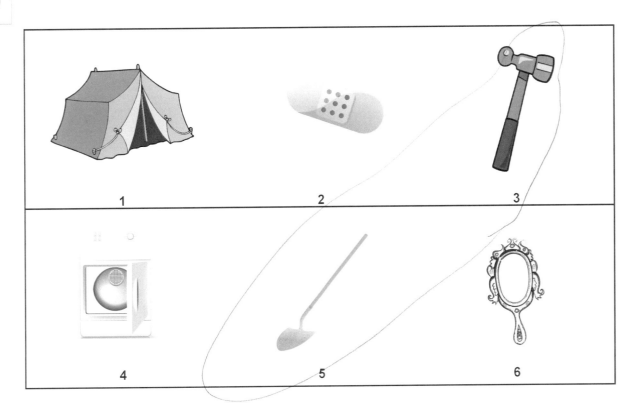

1   2   3

4   5   6

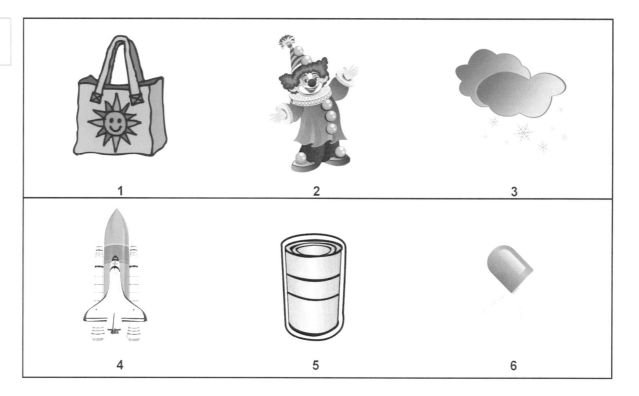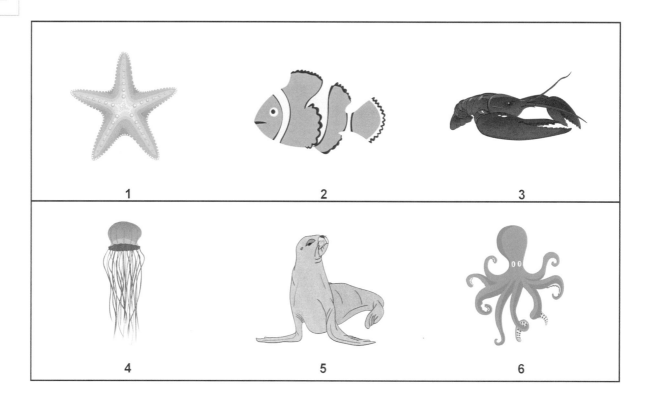

11

1 2 3
4 5 6

12

1 2 3
4 5 6

13

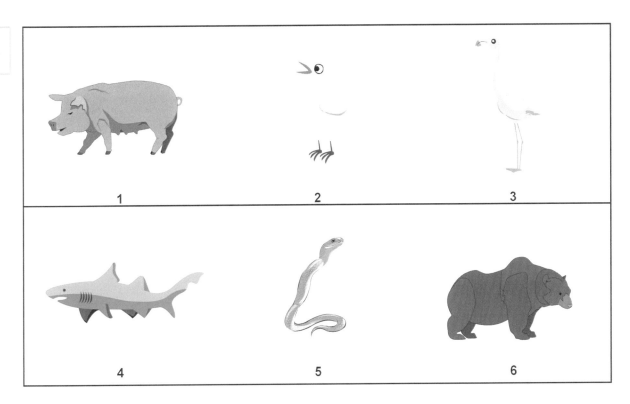

1
2
3
4
5
6

14

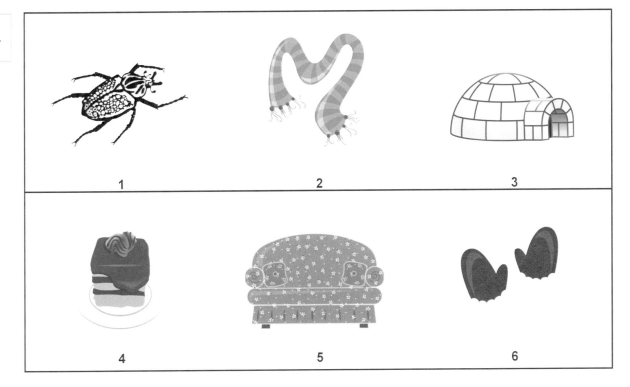

1
2
3
4
5
6

15

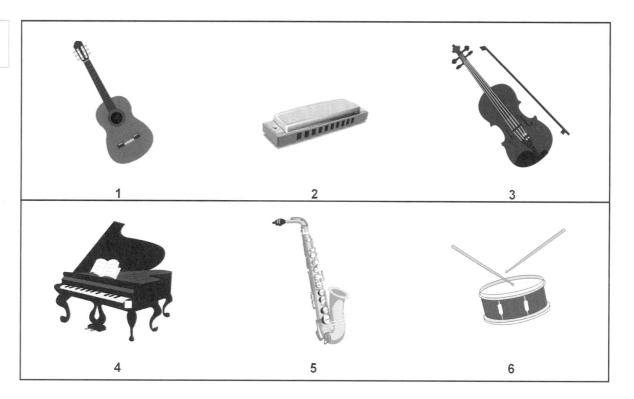

1   2   3

4   5   6

16

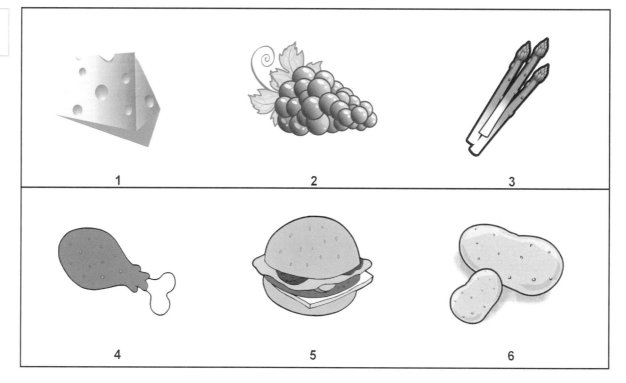

1   2   3

4   5   6

17

1

2

3

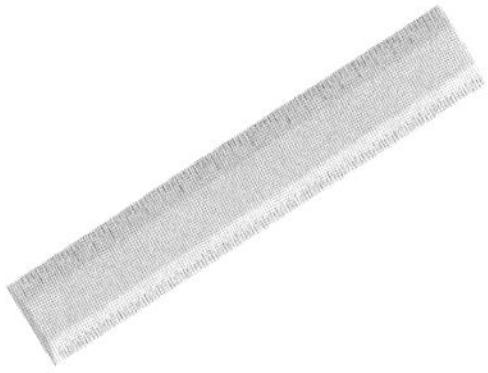

4

5

6

7

8

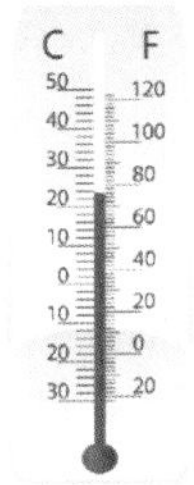

9

18

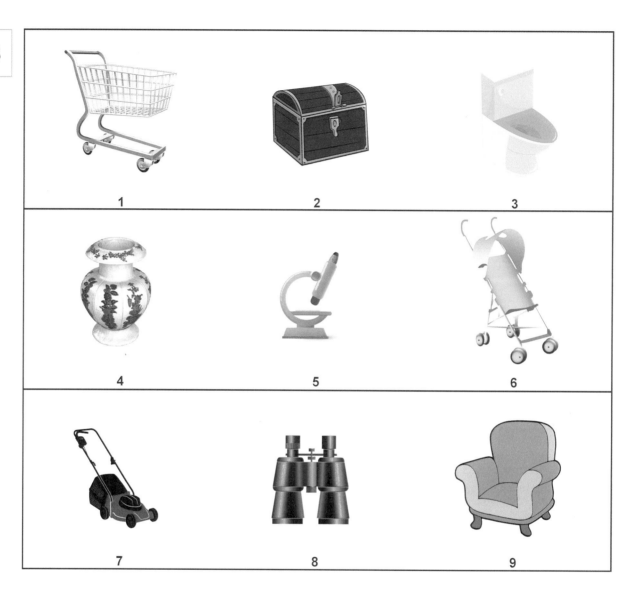

1

2

3

4

5

6

7

8

9

19

1

2

3

4

5

6

7

8

9

20

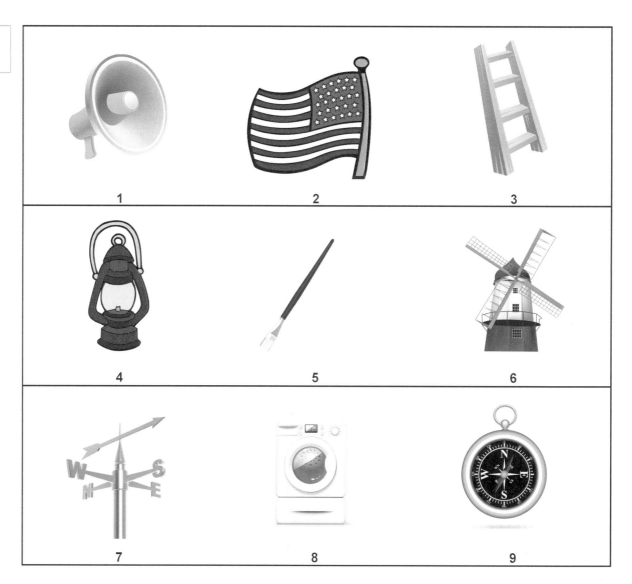

1

2

3

4

5

6

7

8

9

21

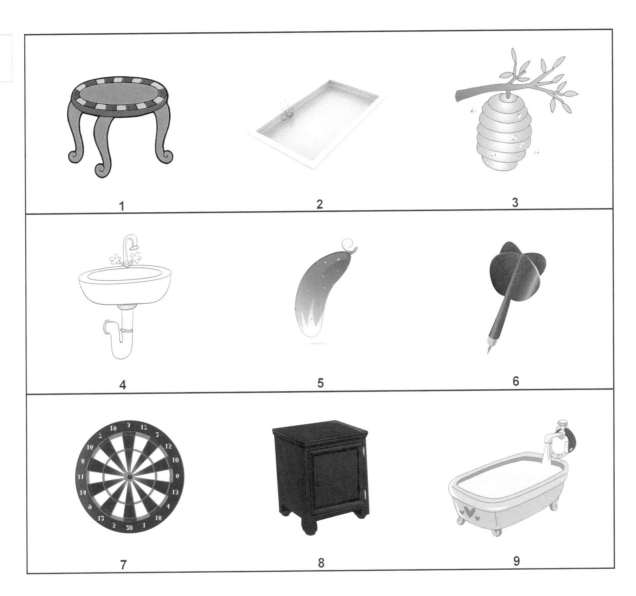

1

2

3

4

5

6

7

8

9

22

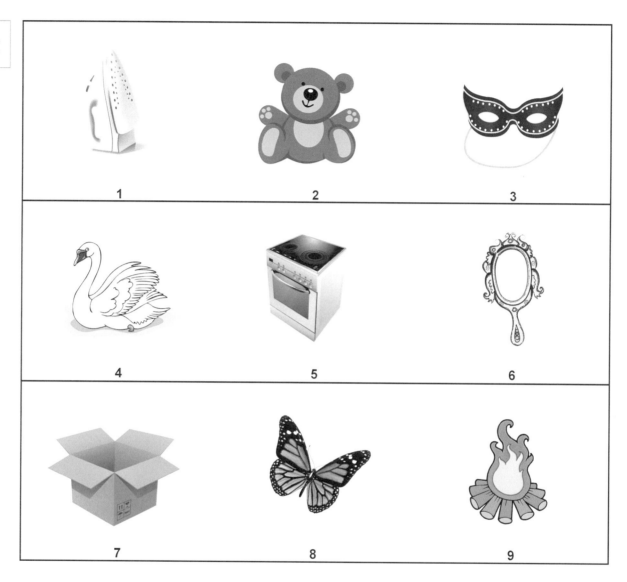

1

2

3

4

5

6

7

8

9

23

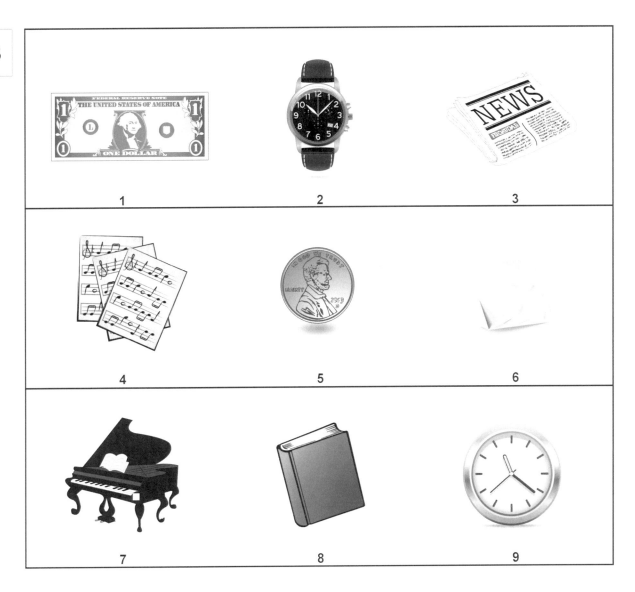

1	2	3
4	5	6
7	8	9

24

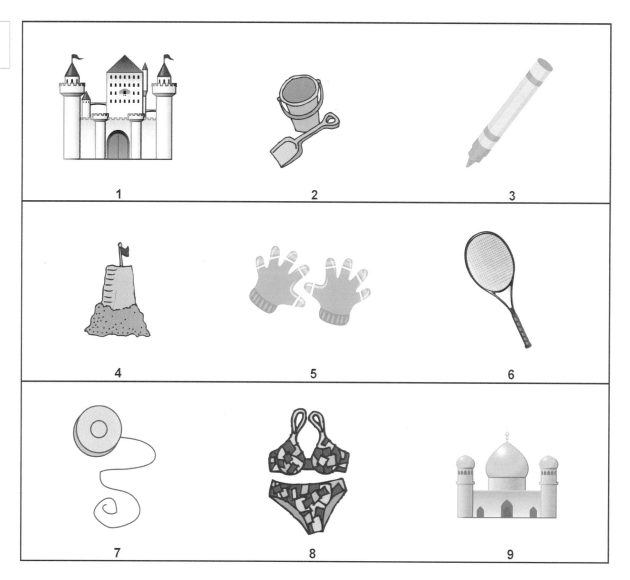

1

2

3

4

5

6

7

8

9

25

1

2

3

4

5

6

7

8

9

26

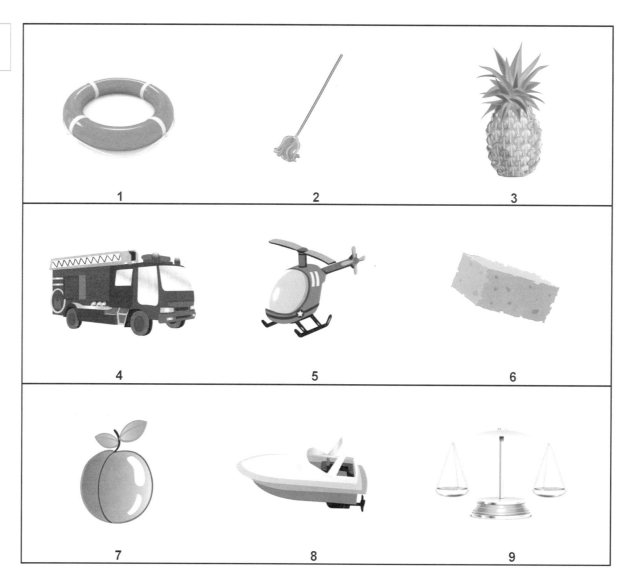

1

2

3

4

5

6

7

8

9

27

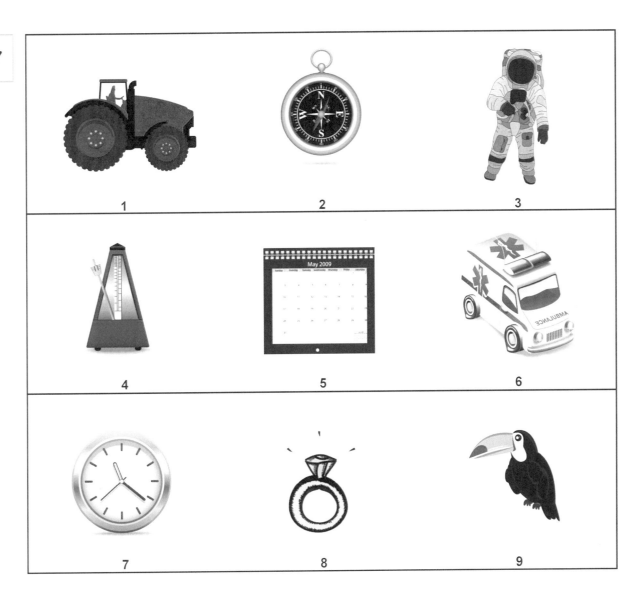

1

2

3

4

5

6

7

8

9

28

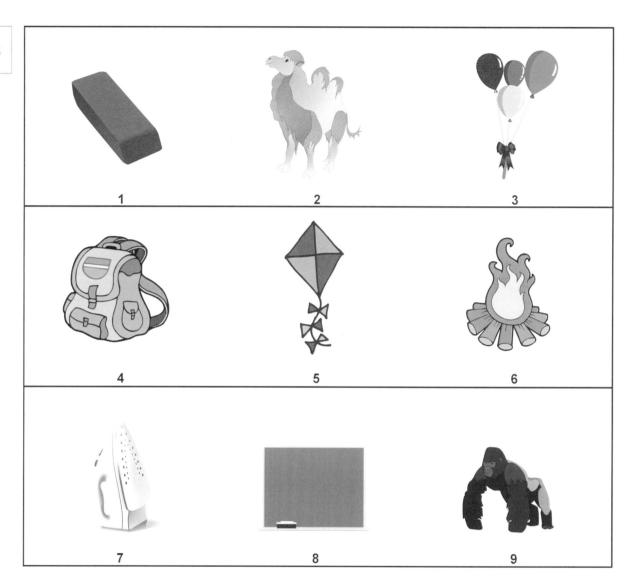

1

2

3

4

5

6

7

8

9

29

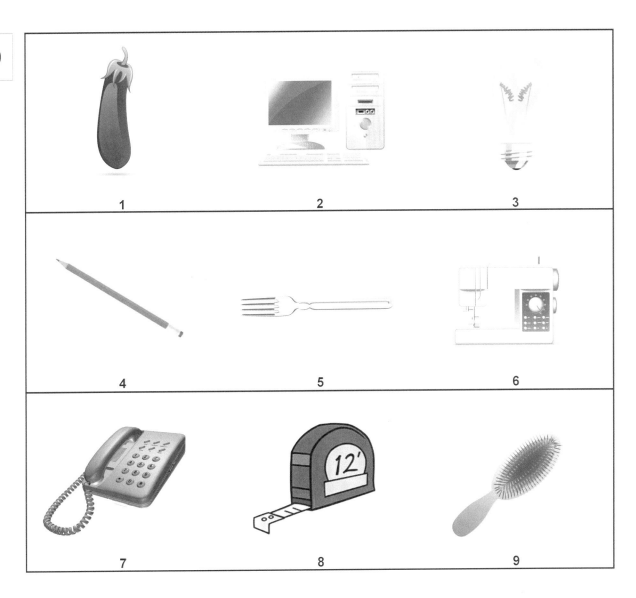

1

2

3

4

5

6

7

8

9

30

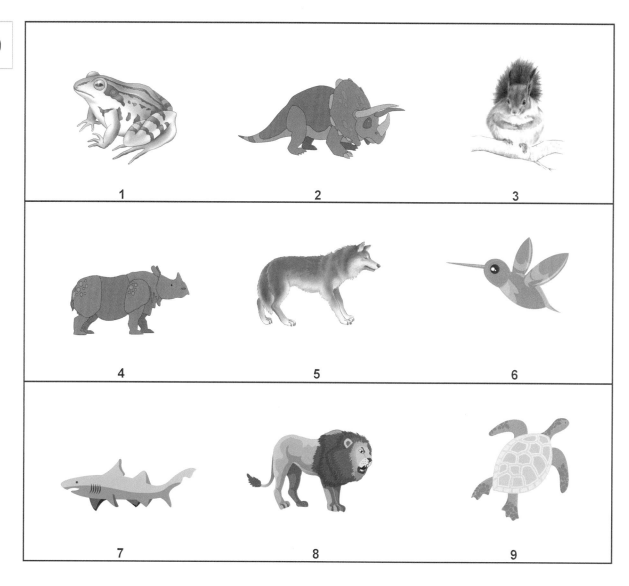

1

2

3

4

5

6

7

8

9

Picture Concepts

Picture	Answer	Category
1	1,4	Animals
2	1,4	Toys
3	2,3	2 Wheels
4	1,4	Insects
5	1,4	Transportation
6	2,3	Can fly
7	1,4	Gives light
8	2,3	Plants
9	1,6	Sports
10	3,5	Tools
11	1,5	Containers
12	2,5	Fins
13	1,6	4 Legs
14	2,6	Worn in cold
15	2,5	Things you blow

Picture	Answer	Category
16	3,6	Vegetables
17	2,4,9	Measuring tools
18	1,6,7	Things you push
19	3,4,9	Things you climb
20	2,6,7	Blow in wind
21	2,4,9	Hold water
22	1,5,9	Things that are hot
23	3,4,8	Things you read
24	2,4,8	Beach related
25	2,4,9	Spins
26	1,6,8	Floats
27	2,5,7	Give information
28	1,4,8	School related
29	2,4,7	Communication
30	3,5,8	Has fur

Description

During the figure weights subtest, your child will view a scale with missing weights and select the response that balances the scale. To answer these questions correctly, your child will match the shapes, and/or apply mathematical concepts.

Instructions

Begin children of all ages at exercise one. For each exercise say:

> **"Which one of these** (point to the answer choices) **weighs the same as this** (point to the left side of the scale)?"

Time answer choices 1-10 for 20 seconds. Questions 11-48 should be timed for 30 seconds. The answer key can be found on page 165.

1

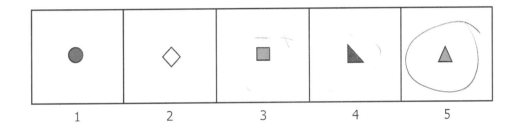

| 1 | 2 | 3 | 4 | 5 |

2

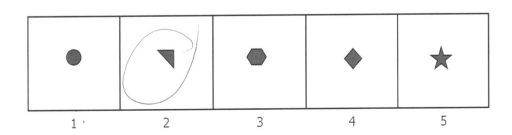

| 1 | 2 | 3 | 4 | 5 |

3

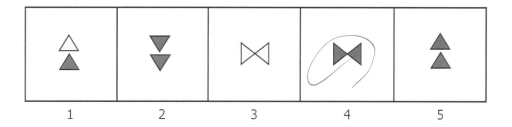

1	2	3	4	5

4

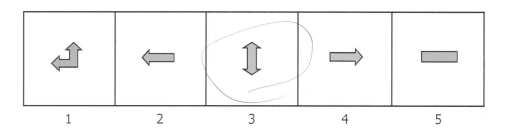

1	2	3	4	5

5

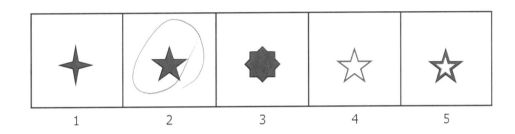

| 1 | 2 | 3 | 4 | 5 |

6

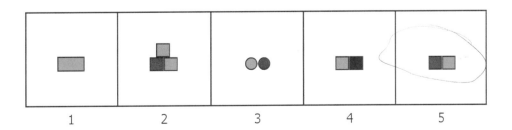

| 1 | 2 | 3 | 4 | 5 |

7

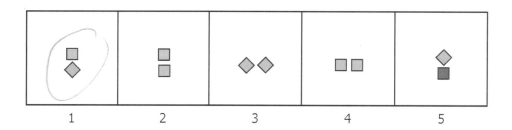

| 1 | 2 | 3 | 4 | 5 |

8

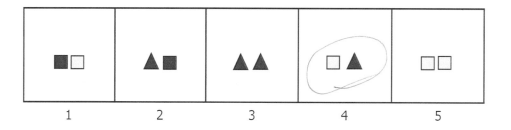

| 1 | 2 | 3 | 4 | 5 |

9

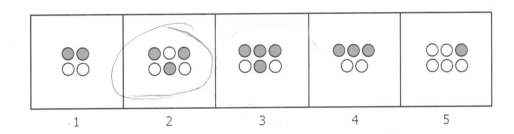

1   2   3   4   5

10

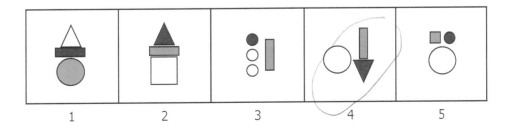

1   2   3   4   5

11

1	2	3	4	5

12

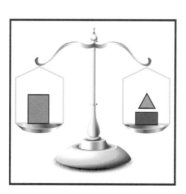 

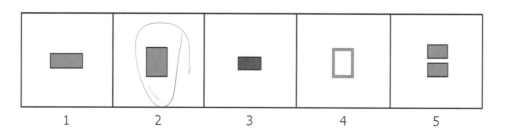

1	2	3	4	5

13

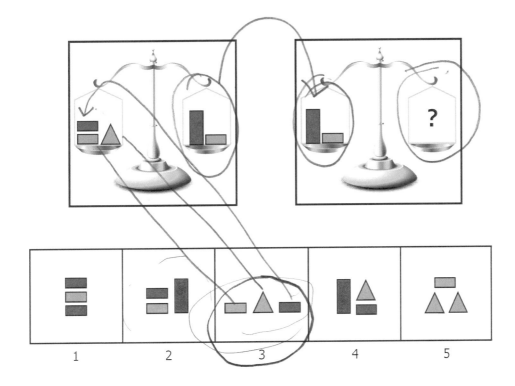

14

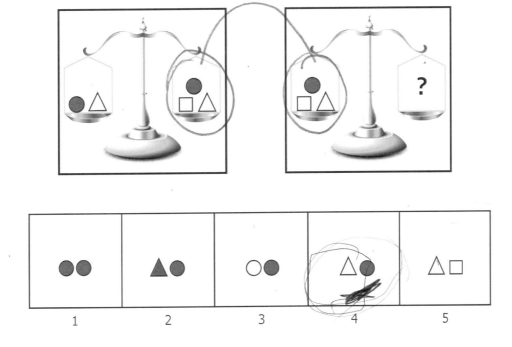

15

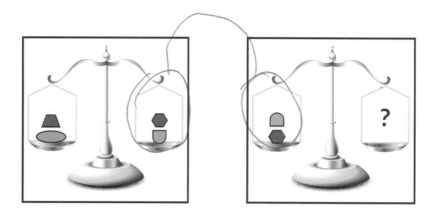

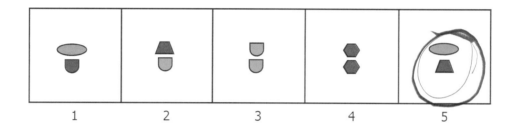

1	2	3	4	5

16

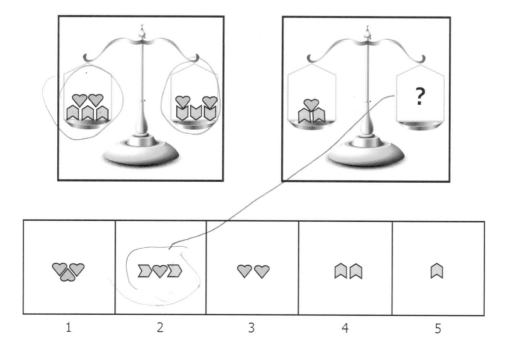

1	2	3	4	5

17

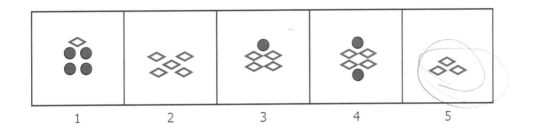

1	2	3	4	5

18

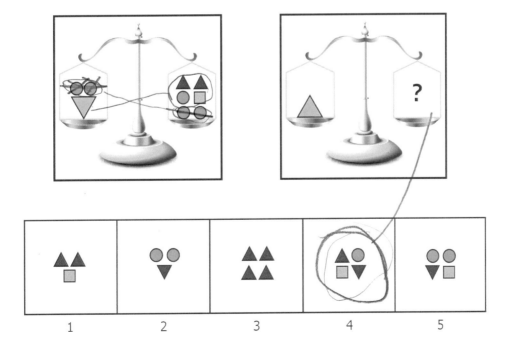

1	2	3	4	5

19

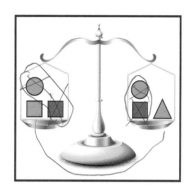 

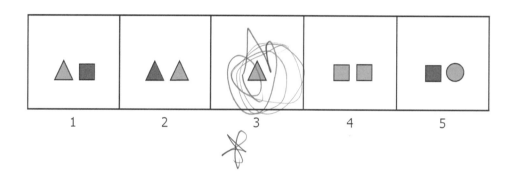

| 1 | 2 | 3 | 4 | 5 |

20

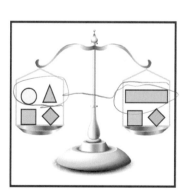 

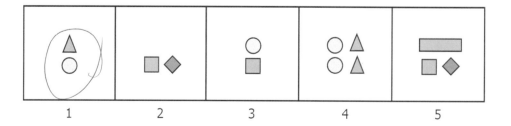

| 1 | 2 | 3 | 4 | 5 |

21

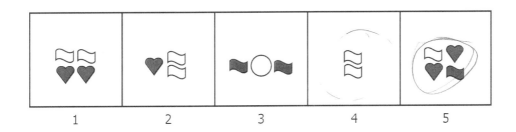

22

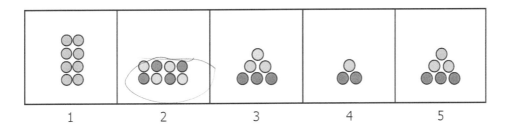

23

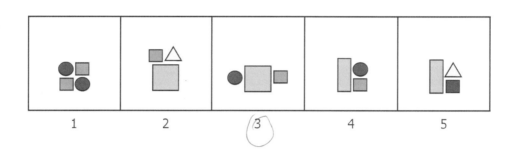

| 1 | 2 | 3 | 4 | 5 |

24

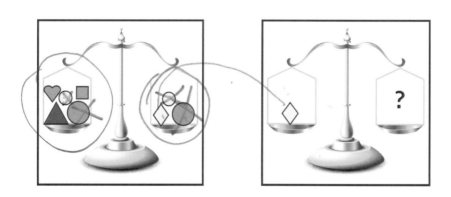

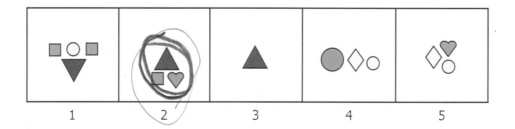

| 1 | 2 | 3 | 4 | 5 |

25

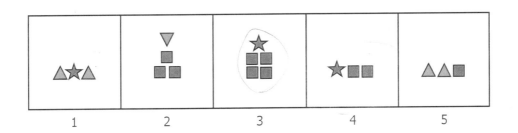

1	2	3	4	5

26

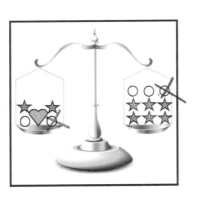 

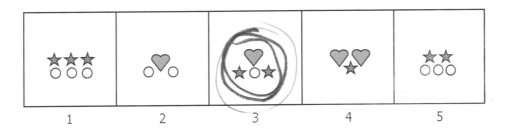

1	2	3	4	5

154

27

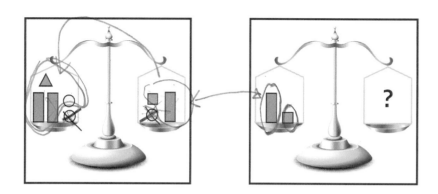

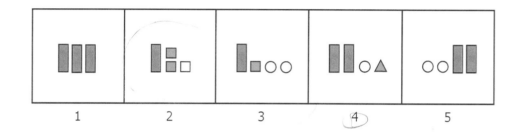

28

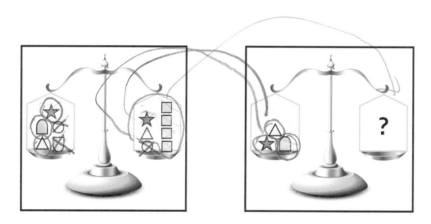

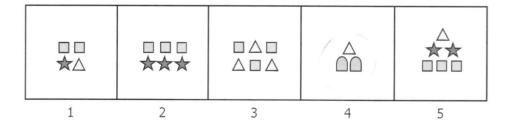

29

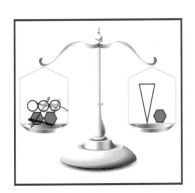 

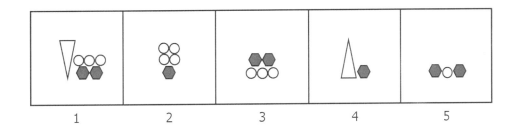

| 1 | 2 | 3 | 4 | 5 |

30

| 1 | 2 | 3 | 4 | 5 |

156

31

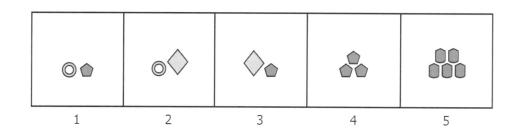

32

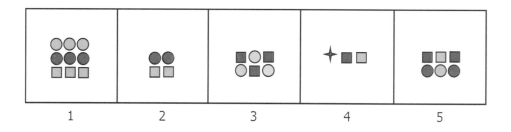

33

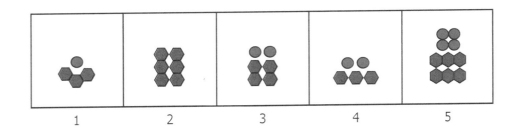

| 1 | 2 | 3 | 4 | 5 |

34

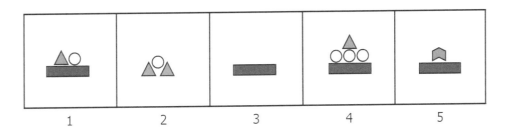

| 1 | 2 | 3 | 4 | 5 |

35

1	2	3	4	5

36

1	2	3	4	5

37

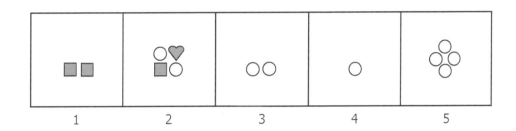

| 1 | 2 | 3 | 4 | 5 |

38

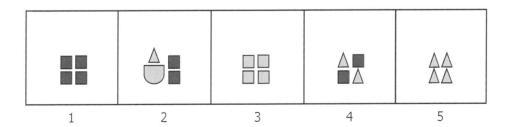

| 1 | 2 | 3 | 4 | 5 |

39

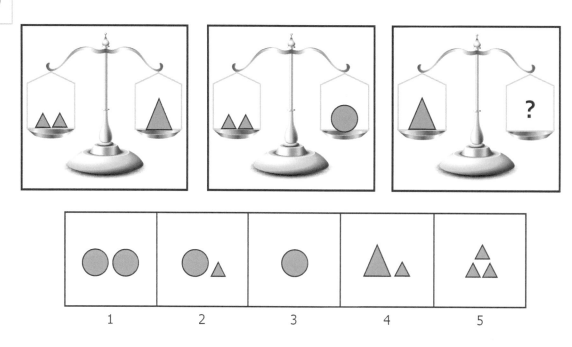

40

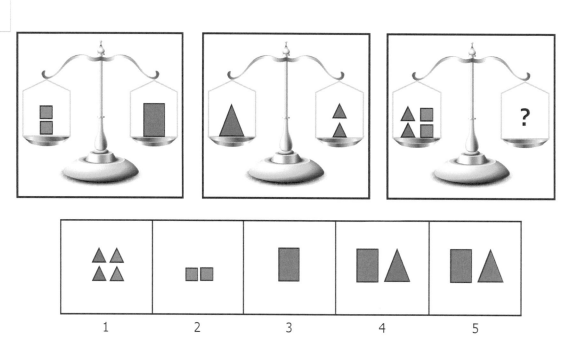

41

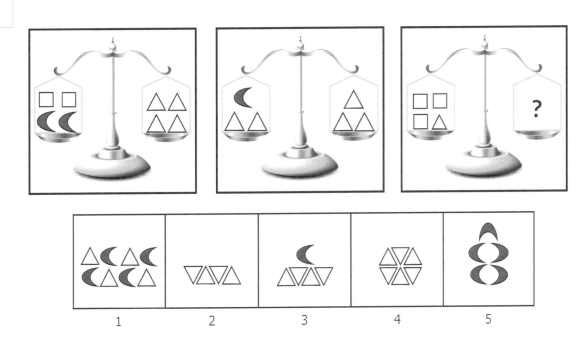

42

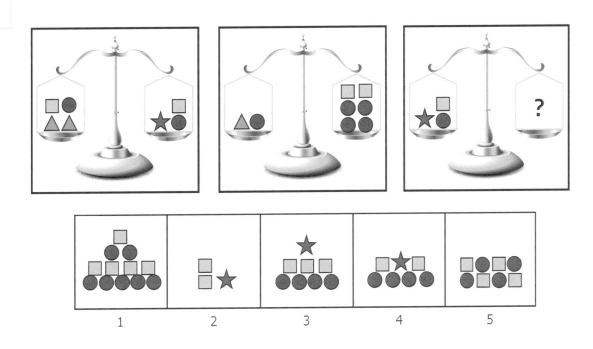

43

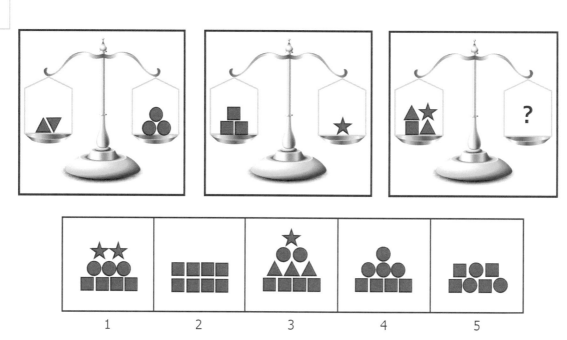

44

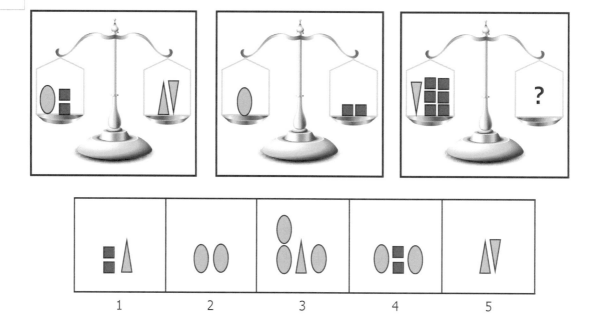

45

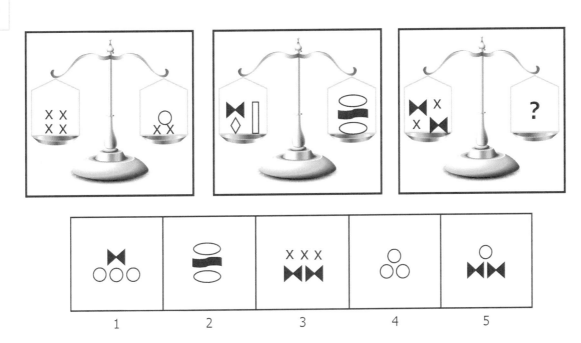

46

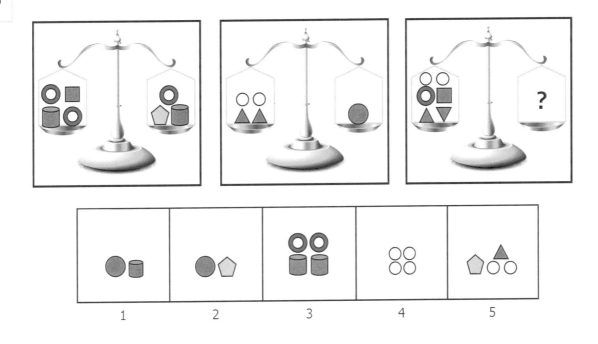

47

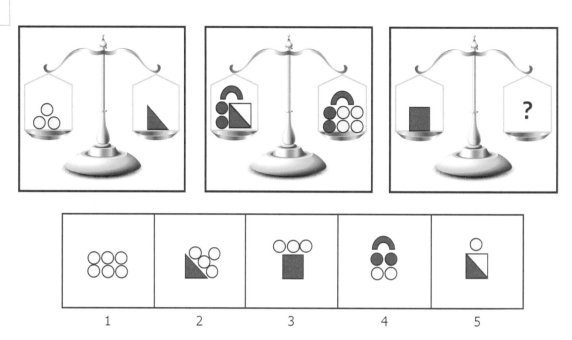

48

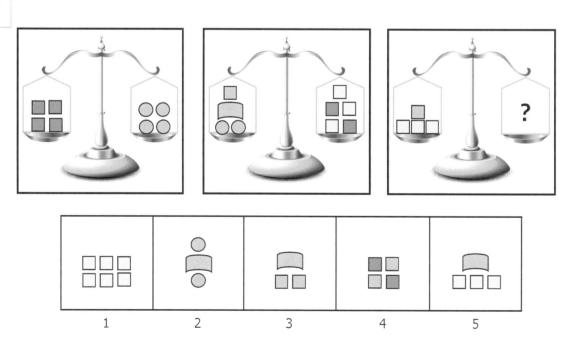

Answer Key

1

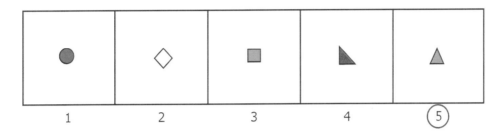

| 1 | 2 | 3 | 4 | ⑤ |

Exactly the same shape, size, color and position.

2

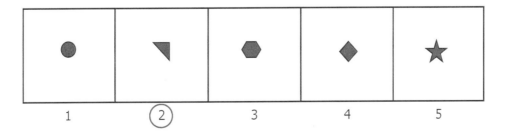

| 1 | ② | 3 | 4 | 5 |

The same shape, size, and color but rotated 180 degrees.

Answer Key

3

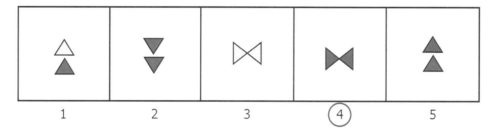

| 1 | 2 | 3 | ④ | 5 |

The same shape, color, and size but rotated 90 degrees.

4

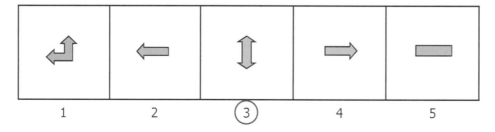

| 1 | 2 | ③ | 4 | 5 |

The same shape, size, and color but rotated 90 degrees.

Answer Key

5

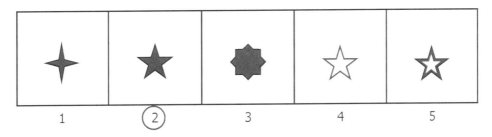

| 1 | ② | 3 | 4 | 5 |

Exactly the same shape, size, color and position.

6

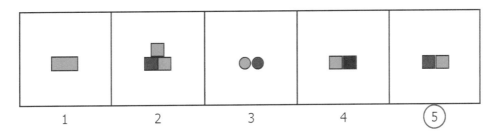

| 1 | 2 | 3 | 4 | ⑤ |

The same shape, size, and color but rotated 180 degrees.

Answer Key

7

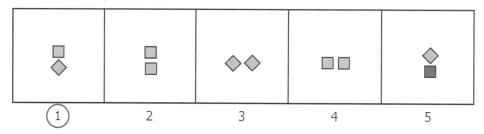

The same shape, color, and size but in different positions.

8

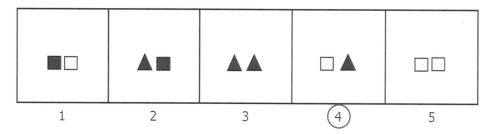

The same shape, size, and color but in different positions.

Answer Key

9

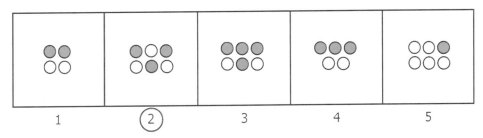

The same shapes, sizes, and colors in a different positional arrangement.

10

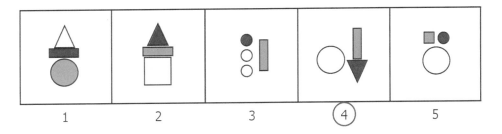

The same shapes, sizes, and colors in a different positional arrangement.

Answer Key

11

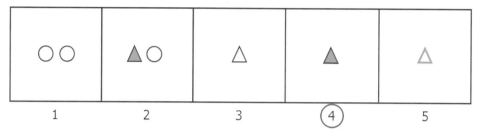

| 1 | 2 | 3 | 4 | 5 |

The green triangle is the same weight as the yellow circle, therefore the yellow circle is the same weight as the green triangle.

12

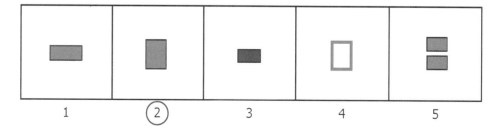

| 1 | 2 | 3 | 4 | 5 |

The orange rectangle is the same weight as the green triangle and the purple rectangle, therefore the green triangle and the purple rectangle are the same weight as the orange rectangle.

Answer Key

13

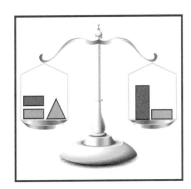 

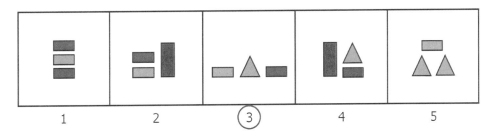

The first set of shapes is equal to the second set of shapes and vice versa.

14

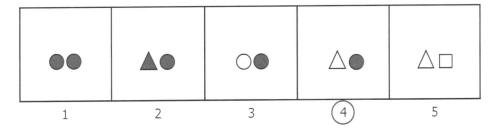

The first set of shapes is equal to the second set of shapes and vice versa.

Answer Key

15

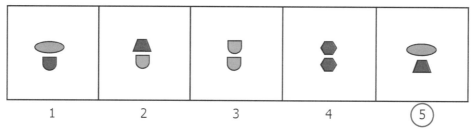

The first set of shapes is equal to the second set of shapes and vice versa. Even if the position of the shapes change, the weight remains the same.

16

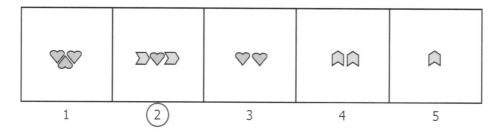

The same shapes in different positions are of equal weight.

Figure Weights

Answer Key

17

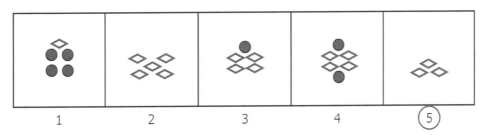

If 6 diamonds = 2 diamonds + 2 circles, then 2 circles = 4 diamonds. Therefore, 1 circle = 2 diamonds. As such, 1 purple circle + 1 diamond = 3 diamonds

18

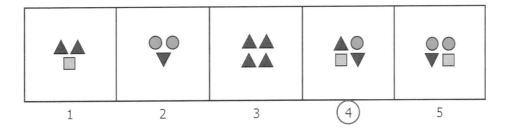

If 1 yellow triangle + 2 green circles = 2 red triangles + 3 green circles + 1 yellow square, then 1 yellow triangle = 2 red triangles + 1 green circle + 1 yellow square.

Answer Key

19

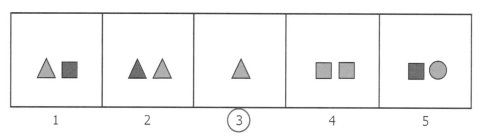

If 1 blue circle + 1 blue square + 1 purple square = 1 blue circle + 1 purple square + 1 blue triangle, then 1 blue square = 1 blue triangle

20

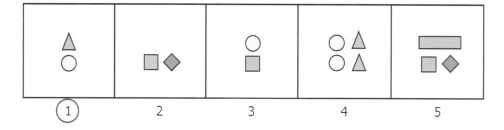

If 1 yellow circle + 1 green triangle + 1 green square + 1 blue diamond = 1 green rectangle + 1 green square + 1 blue diamond, then 1 green rectangle = 1 yellow circle + 1 green triangle.

Answer Key

21

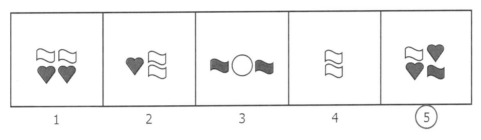

| 1 | 2 | 3 | 4 | ⑤ |

If 2 red hearts + 2 yellow quadrangles + 1 red quadrangle = 1 yellow circle + 1 yellow quadrangle + 1 red triangle, then 1 yellow circle + 1 red triangle = 2 red hearts + 1 yellow quadrangle + 1 red quadrangle.

22

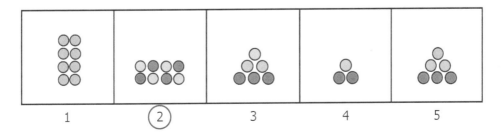

| 1 | ② | 3 | 4 | 5 |

The first scale shows that 1 pink circle = 1 green circle + 1 orange circle. Therefore, 4 pink circles = 4 green circles + 4 orange circles

Answer Key

23

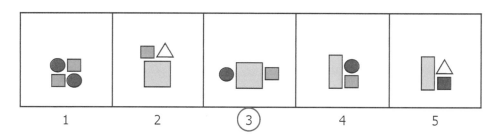

| 1 | 2 | ③ | 4 | 5 |

The same shapes in a different arrangement.

24

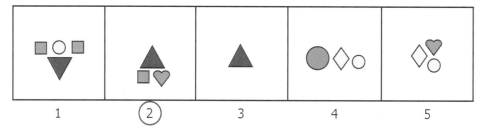

| 1 | ② | 3 | 4 | 5 |

1 heart + 1 yellow circle + 1 square + 1 triangle + 1 green circle = 1 yellow circle + 1 green circle + 1 diamond. Therefore, 1 diamond = 1 triangle + 1 square + 1 heart

Answer Key

25

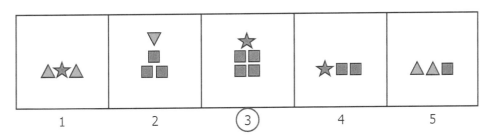

| 1 | 2 | ③ | 4 | 5 |

From the first scale we can deduce that 1 blue triangle = 2 orange squares + 1 orange star. Therefore 1 blue triangle + 2 orange squares = 4 orange squares + 1 orange star.

26

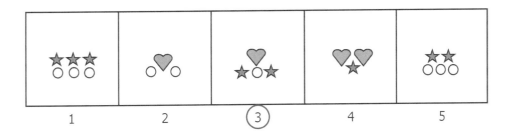

| 1 | 2 | ③ | 4 | 5 |

The first scale shows that 1 blue heart = 1 yellow circle + 4 orange stars. Therefore 6 orange stars + 2 yellow circles = 1 blue heart + 2 orange stars + 1 yellow circle.

Answer Key

27

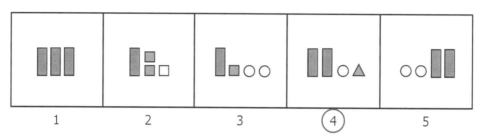

From the first scale we can deduce that 1 blue square = 1 blue triangle + 1 orange rectangle + 1 yellow circle. Therefore 1 orange rectangle + 1 blue square = 1 orange rectangle + 1 blue triangle + 1 orange rectangle + 1 yellow circle. So the answer is 2 orange rectangles + 1 blue triangle + 1 yellow circle.

28

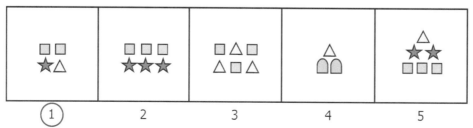

From the first scale we can deduce that: [symbols] = [squares]   Therefore: [symbols]

Answer Key

29

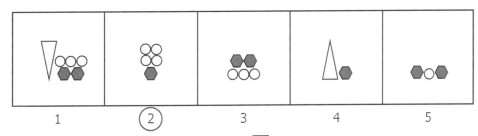

From the first scale we can deduce that: ⬛ = ⬡ ○○○   Therefore: ⬛ ○ = ⬡ ○○○○

30

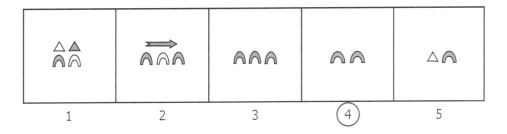

The same shape, size, and color but in different positions.

Answer Key

31

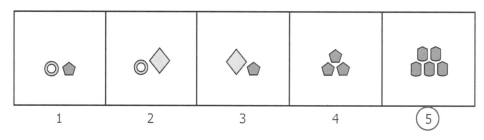

The same shapes, color, quantity and size.

32

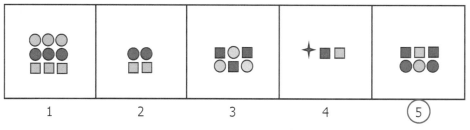

Answer Key

33

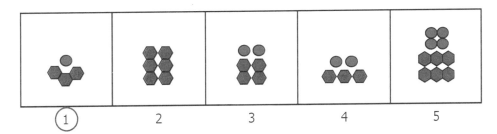

① 2 3 4 5

From the first scale we can deduce that: ⬡ = ●● Therefore: [figure] = [figure]

34

1 2 ③ 4 5

Here's how to solve this: = Therefore: ▬ = ○ △

Answer Key

35

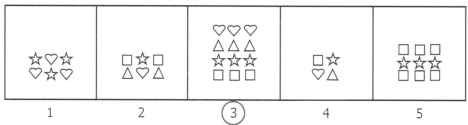

From the first scale we can deduce that: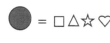

36

Answer Key

37

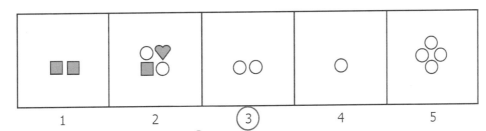

1	2	3	4	5

Here's how to solve this: Therefore:

38

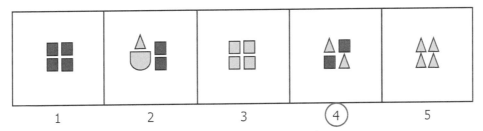

1	2	3	4	5

From the first scale we can deduce that:

Answer Key

39

 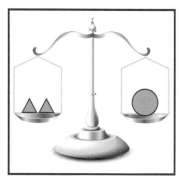 

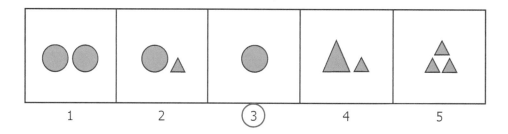

2 small blue triangles = 1 large blue triangle and 2 small blue triangles = 1 large blue circle. Therefore, 1 large blue triangle = 1 large blue circle

40

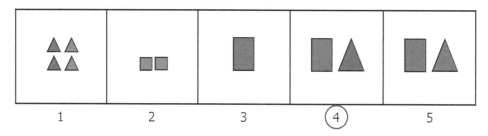

2 small orange squares = 1 large orange rectangle. 1 large brown triangle = 2 small brown triangles. Therefore, 2 small brown triangles + 2 small orange squares = 1 large orange rectangle + 1 large brown triangle.

Answer Key

41

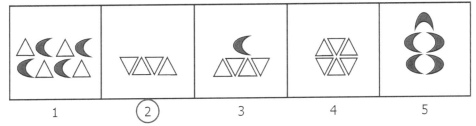

From the second scale we can deduce that ☾ = △ Therefore, from the first scale we can deduce that:

□□ = □□ = △△
☾☾   △△   △△

So □□ = △△ and □ = △

Therefore □□ = △△
         □△   △△

42

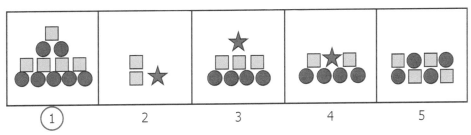

From the first scale we can deduce that 1 star = 2 triangles. From the second scale we can deduce that 1 triangle = 3 circles and 2 squares. Therefore 1 star + 1 square + 1 circle = 2 triangles + 1 square + 1 circle. Which is also equal to 7 circles + 5 squares.

Answer Key

43

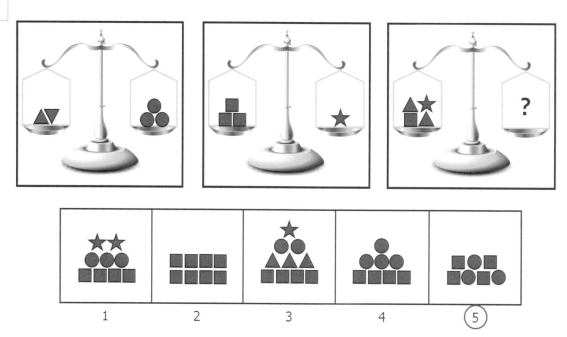

2 triangles = 3 circles. 1 star = 3 squares. Therefore 2 triangles + 1 star + 1 square = 3 circles + 3 squares + 1 square. Which is the same as 3 circles + 4 squares.

44

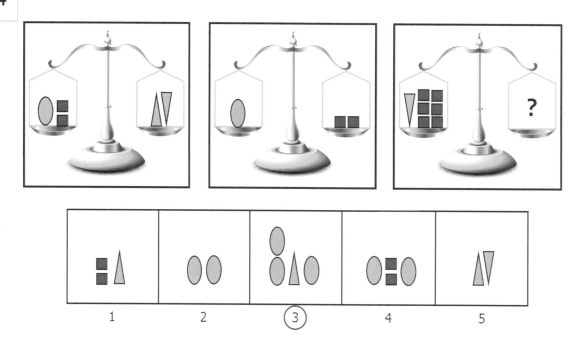

In the second scale we see that 1 oval = 2 squares. So, 6 squares = 3 ovals. 6 squares + 1 triangle = 3 ovals + 1 triangle

Answer Key

45

 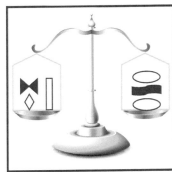 

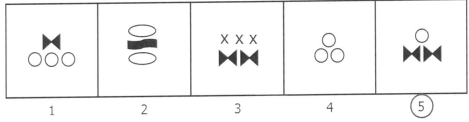

From the first scale we can deduce that ◯ = x + x Therefore x + x + ◧ + ◨ = ◯ + ◧ + ◨

46

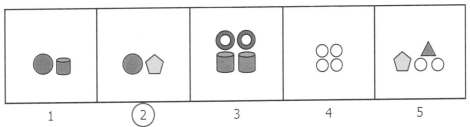

From the first scale we can deduce that: ◯ ■ = ⬠ From the second scale we can see that:

47

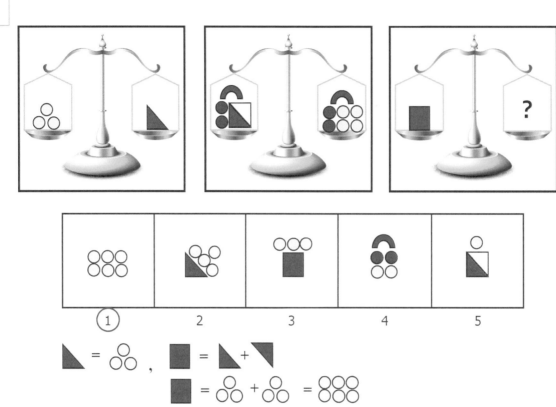

48

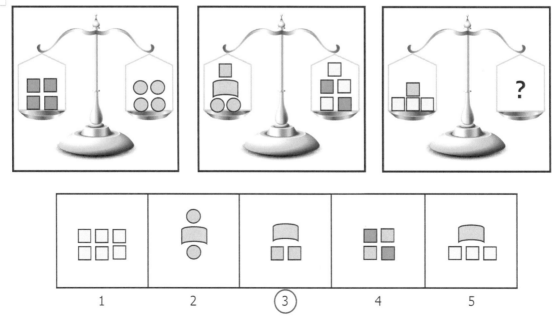

From the first scale we can deduce that ▨ = ◯. From the second scale we can deduce that

▨◠ = ☐☐☐ Therefore, ☐▨☐ = ☐☐◠

Description:

The arithmetic subtest is administered in 2 parts:

Picture Items:
Your child will be asked to solve math problems involving pictures.

Verbal Items:
After the examiner reads arithmetic problems, your child will be asked to mentally solve them within 30 seconds. Each correct answer will receive 1 point.

PICTURE ITEMS

Instructions:

Children age 6-8 should start with question #1.
Children ages 9 and up should skip the picture items and start with verbal item #1.
Begin by saying: **"Now I'd like for you to solve a few math problems."** Read the questions and write down your child's response. The answer key for the picture items is on page 194.

VERBAL ITEMS

Instructions:

Say: **"Now I'd like you to solve some math problems."** Read each math problem to your child. Allow 30 seconds for a response.

| 1 | Which box has 4 dogs? |

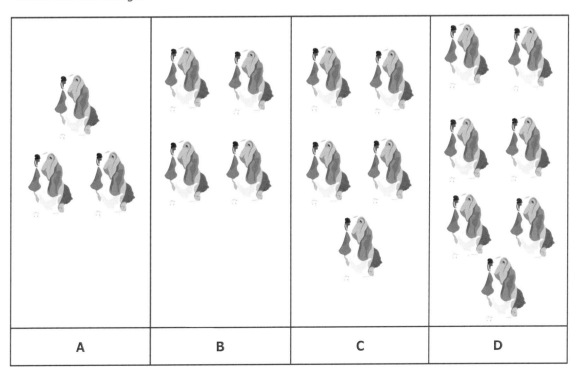

| A | B | C | D |

2   Sally has the number of apples shown in the box. She has twice as many apples as pears. How many pears does she have?

3   Thirteen children want to ride bicycles but the bike shop only has the number of bikes shown in the box. How many children will not have a bike to ride?

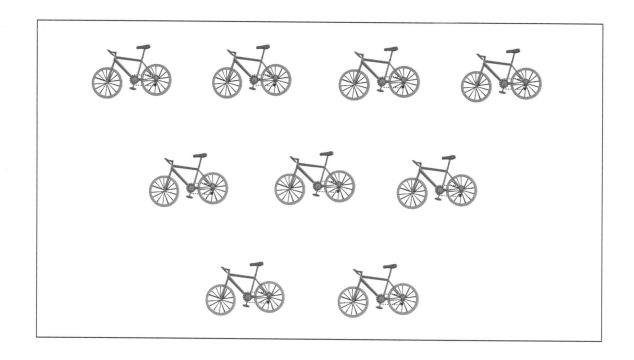

4

How many more fish are there than seahorses?

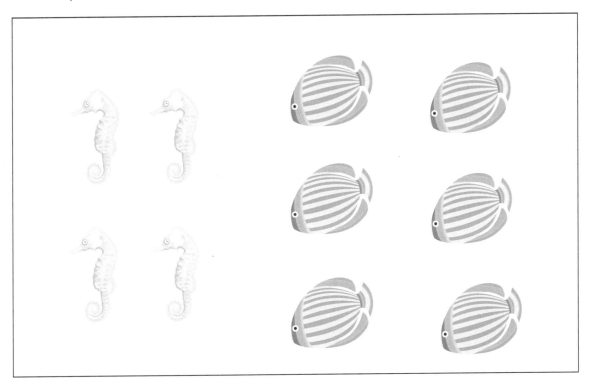

5

If only one bird can fit into a birdhouse, how many birds will be without a home?

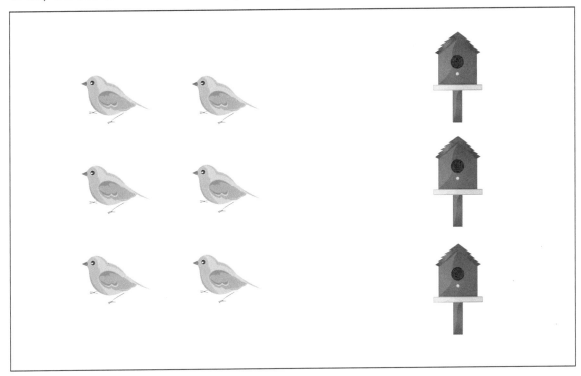

6 How many more basketballs do we need in order to have an equal number of baseballs and basketballs?

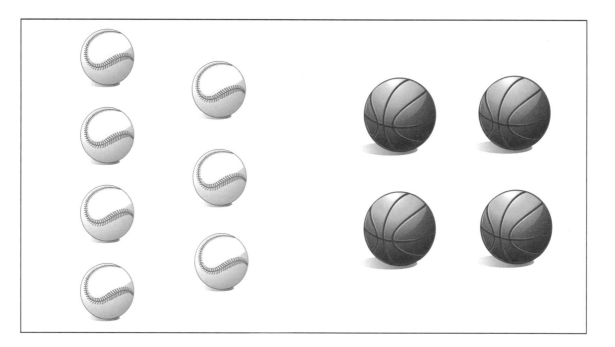

7 If each rabbit eats 2 carrots, how many carrots will be left?

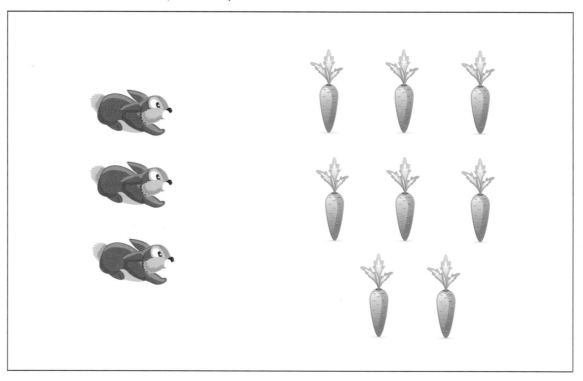

8   If each chimp eats 2 bananas, how many will be left?

9   If each airplane needs 2 pilots, how many more pilots are needed to fly all of the airplanes?

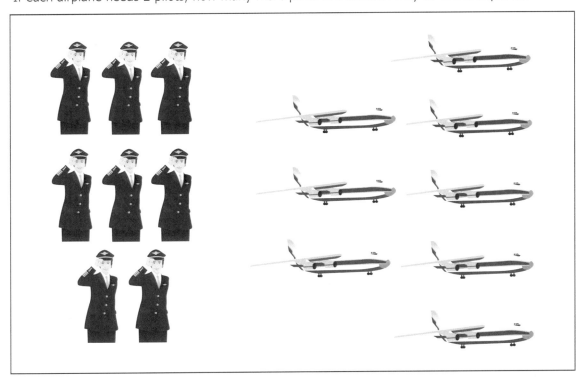

Picture Arithmetic Answer Key			
1. Dogs	B	6. Balls	3
2. Apples	3	7. Rabbits	2
3. Bicycles	4	8. Chimps	6
4. Seahorses & Fish	2	9. Pilots	8
5. Birds	3		

1. Jane has 4 jellybeans. Her mother gives her 1 more. How many jelly beans does she have now? (5)

2. Chris has 6 pieces of gum. He loses 1 piece. How many pieces of gum does he have left? (5)

3. How many are 3 apples and 3 oranges? (6)

4. Susan has 4 cupcakes. She gives 1 to Beth, 1 to Laura and 1 to her brother. How many cupcakes does she have left? (1)

5. How many are 4 crayons and 2 pencils? (6)

6. Mom cut an orange in half. She gave Charlie 1 piece and Rachel another piece. How many pieces did Danny get? (0)

7. If I cut a cookie in thirds, how many pieces will I have? (3)

8. If you have 5 pennies in each hand, how many pennies do you have? (10)

9. Matthew has 3 toy cars and his friend Bill gives him 4 more for his birthday. How many toy cars does Matthew have now? (7)

10. Sally has 3 lemons. To make lemonade she needs 10 lemons. How many more lemons does she need? (7)

11. Jack collects 4 sea shells from the beach. He later loses 2 but collects 6 more. How many shells does he have left? (8)

12. Olivia has to climb 20 stairs to get to her apartment. She has already climbed 15 stairs, how many more stairs does she need to climb to get home? (5)

13. There are 8 lighted candles on Jane's birthday cake. She blows out 6. How many are still lighted? (2)

14. Stanley buys 10 pencils at 1 store and 18 pencils at another. How many pencils does he have all together? (28)

15. Chris is at the bus stop. There are 7 people on the bus. Three people get off of the bus. Two other people get on. How many people are on the bus now? (6)

16. Billy's mom gave him $15.00. Stickers cost 50 cents a sheet. How many sheets of stickers can Billy buy? (30)

17. Karen earns $2 for each chore. She completed 8 chores this week. Her father paid her $15. How much more money does her father owe her? ($1)

18. Louis bought a hat for $5, a toy for $3 and a coloring book for $1.50. How much change should she get back for a $10 bill? (50 cents)

19. Sally has 25 flower pots. She has 400 seeds to plant. How many seeds should she put in each pot? (16)

20. Max is having a yard sale. He sells 3 pairs of pants for $3 each, a lamp for $25 dollars, and 2 toy trains for $2 each to his neighbor. His neighbor gives him $40. How much change should Max give his neighbor? ($2)

21. Carlos is twice as old as Robert. Robert is 15 years old. How old is Carlos? (30)

22. A school's basketball team played 10 games last year. They scored 10 points in 4 of the games and they scored 5 points in 6 of the games. What is the average number of points the team scored in each game? (7)

23. Between 1980 and 1985, the lemonade stand's sales rose from $50 a year to $60 a year. Between 1985 and 1990, sales rose from $60 to $70 a year. On average, how much did sales rise each year? ($2)

24. Sue bought 9 brownies from the store. She ate 2/3 of them. How many did she eat? (6)

25. Bob bought a bicycle at a 25% discount. He paid $60 for it. What was the original price? ($80)

26. It takes 4 bakers to bake 50 cakes in 5 days. How many bakers would it take to bake 40 cakes in 12 hours? (32)

27. Sue bought a book that normally sells for $15 at a 20% discount. How much did Sue pay for the book on sale? ($12)

28. It takes 2 carpenters 30 days to build 12 bookcases. How many carpenters are needed to build 60 bookcases in 15 days? (20)

29. Train A departs for Boston at 8 a.m. travelling at 50 mph. Train B departs for Boston at 10 a.m. travelling at 60 mph. How far behind is Train B 4 hours after Train A departs? (80 miles)

Description

This subtest is administered in three parts:

Digit Span Forward: The child recites a series of numbers in the order spoken by the examiner.

Digit Span Backward: The child recites a series of numbers in the reverse order spoken by the examiner.

Digit Span Sequencing: The child recites a series of numbers in order of smallest to biggest.

DIGIT SPAN FORWARD

Instructions

Say: **"I will say some numbers. When I'm finished, I want you to repeat them. Let's start with..."**

Forward Exercises	
1) 1-7	17) 1-4-2-8-6-9
2) 6-3	18) 5-7-3-9-1-4
3) 3-5	19) 8-2-3-5-9-1
4) 8-2	20) 4-1-8-9-5-6
5) 2-7-4	21) 6-8-1-2-7-3-4
6) 1-3-6	22) 5-9-3-4-6-2-1
7) 4-3-1	23) 8-5-9-1-7-6-2
8) 9-2-3	24) 2-1-5-7-9-3-4
9) 2-3-6-8	25) 7-2-4-3-1-5-8-6
10) 1-5-2-6	26) 5-1-9-6-3-7-4-8
11) 5-0-4-7	27) 1-5-6-2-3-7-9-8
12) 9-8-3-4	28) 3-8-2-7-5-2-6-1
13) 1-5-3-9-6	29) 9-4-1-7-6-5-2-3-8
14) 3-4-1-2-5	30) 3-8-9-2-5-6-4-1-6
15) 9-2-5-7-3	31) 8-1-3-6-9-2-5-4-7
16) 7-5-6-3-1	32) 1-5-7-2-4-3-9-6-8

DIGIT SPAN BACKWARD

Instructions

Say: "Now I will say some numbers. But now I need you to repeat them backward. So if I say 1-2, you should say 2-1, Okay? Let's start with..."

Backward Exercises	Answer	Backward Exercises	Answer
1) 3-1	1-3	15) 3-9-1-4-7-8	8-7-4-1-9-3
2) 1-2	2-1	16) 4-2-8-9-3-5	5-3-9-8-2-4
3) 4-1-7	7-1-4	17) 5-1-7-4-8-2-3	3-2-8-4-7-1-5
4) 2-3-5	5-3-2	18) 2-4-5-9-3-7-1	1-7-3-9-5-4-2
5) 8-6-1-2	2-1-6-8	19) 6-8-9-1-4-3-6	6-3-4-1-9-8-6
6) 4-9-3-5	5-3-9-4	20) 7-5-2-9-8-1-4	4-1-8-9-2-5-7
7) 2-1-8-3	3-8-1-2	21) 8-9-1-6-2-7-5-3	3-5-7-2-6-1-9-8
8) 1-9-4-3	3-4-9-1	22) 3-4-1-9-2-8-7-6	6-7-8-2-9-1-4-3
9) 5-2-6-7-3	3-7-6-2-5	23) 1-8-5-2-3-7-5-9	9-5-7-3-2-5-8-1
10) 3-4-8-1-9	9-1-8-4-3	24) 5-4-3-8-9-1-7-2	2-7-1-9-8-3-4-5
11) 7-2-1-3-5	5-3-1-2-7	25) 4-7-3-5-1-8-2-9-6	6-9-2-8-1-5-3-7-4
12) 4-5-9-6-3	3-6-9-5-4	26) 9-7-2-5-8-1-3-2-4	4-2-3-1-8-5-2-7-9
13) 1-8-3-4-7-9	9-7-4-3-8-1	27) 2-8-6-9-4-3-7-1-5	5-1-7-3-4-9-6-8-2
14) 2-5-4-6-8-1	1-8-6-4-5-2	28) 7-1-9-4-8-3-5-2-6	6-2-5-3-8-4-9-1-7

DIGIT SPAN SEQUENCING

Instructions

Say: "**Now I will say some numbers. This time I need you to repeat them to me from the smallest number to the biggest number. So if I say 3-2-1, you should say 1-2-3, Okay? Let's start with…**"

Sequencing Exercises	Answer	Sequencing Exercises	Answer
1) 9-1	1-9	22) 5-9-6-3-8-0	0-3-5-6-8-9
2) 7-2	2-7	23) 7-2-4-3-8-1	1-2-3-4-7-8
3) 6-4	4-6	24) 9-4-6-1-8-7	1-4-6-7-8-9
4) 8-7	7-8	25) 8-5-2-3-7-9-1	1-2-3-5-7-8-9
5) 7-5-3	3-5-7	26) 1-8-5-0-4-2-3	0-1-2-3-4-5-8
6) 6-8-2	2-6-8	27) 6-8-7-1-5-3-4	1-3-4-5-6-7-8
7) 4-2-1	1-2-4	28) 3-9-0-1-7-2-6	0-1-2-3-6-7-9
8) 5-2-6	2-5-6	29) 5-4-2-3-7-8-1	1-2-3-4-5-7-8
9) 9-7-4	4-7-9	30) 2-4-3-8-5-6-9	2-3-4-5-6-8-9
10) 6-8-4-2	2-4-6-8	31) 7-1-8-6-3-4-0-5	0-1-3-4-5-6-7-8
11) 8-6-7-0	0-6-7-8	32) 8-2-5-6-4-9-0-3	0-2-3-4-5-6-8-9
12) 9-8-5-4	4-5-8-9	33) 3-1-5-0-2-7-4-8	0-1-2-3-4-5-7-8
13) 1-8-7-3	1-3-7-8	34) 1-3-4-5-8-6-9-2	1-2-3-4-5-6-8-9
14) 5-3-9-2	2-3-5-9	35) 4-1-9-3-8-2-7-6	1-2-3-4-6-7-8-9
15) 8-6-9-2-4	2-4-6-8-9	36) 9-5-6-7-4-3-2-8	2-3-4-5-6-7-8-9
16) 6-9-0-3-4	0-3-4-6-9	37) 2-0-7-6-4-3-8-1-9	0-1-2-3-4-6-7-8-9
17) 5-2-9-7-4	2-4-5-7-9	38) 5-7-2-1-8-4-6-9-0	0-1-2-4-5-6-7-8-9
18) 1-8-3-6-7	1-3-6-7-8	39) 9-2-7-0-3-4-5-1-6	0-1-2-3-4-5-6-7-9
19) 2-1-6-4-3	1-2-3-4-6	40) 4-2-0-7-3-1-8-9-5	0-1-2-3-4-5-7-8-9
20) 4-6-2-0-3-9	0-2-3-4-6-9	41) 3-5-2-6-4-7-9-8-1	1-2-3-4-5-6-7-8-9
21) 0-1-2-8-6-5	0-1-2-5-6-8	42) 1-4-6-3-7-9-0-5-8	0-1-3-4-5-6-7-8-9

Description
During the letter-number subtest, the examiner will read a series of letters and numbers. Your child will be asked to recall the numbers in ascending order and the letters in alphabetical order.

Instructions
Say: **"Let's try another game. When I say a group of numbers and letters, I need you to say the numbers in order beginning with the lowest number. Then say the letters in alphabetical order. For example, if I say B-2, you should say 2-B. Say the number first, then the letter. Let's try the first one..."**

Exercises	Answer	Exercises	Answer
1) 6, B	6, B	21) C, 2, A, 6	2, 6, A, C
2) 2, C	2, C	22) D, 7, L, 9	7, 9, D, L
3) D, 1	1, D	23) 8, E, 3, S	3, 8, E, S
4) F, 2	2, F	24) A, 3, F, 1	1, 3, A, F
5) E, 4	4, E	25) T, 8, K, 6, R	6, 8, K, R, T
6) 3, G	3, G	26) 2, E, 3, F, 9	2, 3, 9, E, F
7) C, 2, 3	2, 3, C	27) D, 5, C, 2, H	2, 5, C, D, H
8) 1, 2, B	1, 2, B	28) 8, N, 5, P, 4	4, 5, 8, N, P
9) A, 3, 2	2, 3, A	29) G, 4, X, 2, I	2, 4, G, I, X
10) J, 2, C	2, C, J	30) 1, P, 9, J, 3	1, 3, 9, J, P
11) M, 2, 6	2, 6, M	31) B, 1, D, 3, R, 7	1, 3, 7, B, D, R
12) D, 4, P	4, D, P	32) 3, C, 5, F, 8, J	3, 5, 8, C, F, J
13) 6, H, 5	5, 6, H	33) K, 1, A, 6, D, 9	1, 6, 9, A, D, K
14) 1, N, B	1, B, N	34) 2, U, 1, D, 4, A	1, 2, 4, A, D, U
15) E, 9, K	9, E, K	35) M, 7, T, 3, W, 1	1, 3, 7, M, T, W
16) 4, G, 2	2, 4, G	36) 9, H, 3, B, 6, C	3, 6, 9, B, C, H
17) 7, 3, A	3, 7, A	37) E, 6, R, 1, A, 4, G	1, 4, 6, A, E, G, R
18) C, 8, D	8, C, D	38) 5, B, 7, G, 3, D, 8	3, 5, 7, 8, B, D, G
19) 4, I, 5, Q	4, 5, I, Q	39) K, 2, N, 1, S, 4, P	1, 2, 4, K, N, P, S
20) 3, B, 1, R	1, 3, B, R	40) 3, C, 2, A, 1, T, 7	1, 2, 3, 7, A, C, T

Exercises	Answer
41) Y, 8, B, 4, F, 1, T	1, 4, 8, B, F, T, Y
42) 9, J, 7, P, 8, S, 4	4, 7, 8, 9, J, P, S
43) B, 5, D, 1, U, 9, E, 2	1, 2, 5, 9, B, D, E, U
44) 8, X, 7, Z, 9, U, 1, G	1, 7, 8, 9, G, U, X, Z
45) L, 7, Y, 8, A, 6, R, 4	4, 6, 7, 8, A, L, R, Y
46) 4, V, 1, N, 9, D, 5, H	1, 4, 5, 9, D, H, N, V
47) I, 2, G, 8, B, 3, W, 7	2, 3, 7, 8, B, G, I, W
48) 2, V, 5, H, 6, R, 4, M	2, 4, 5, 6, H, M, R, V

Picture Span

Description

During the picture span subtest, the examiner will ask your child to look at a set of pictures for a few seconds. After the time has elapsed, the examiner will show your child a new set of pictures. Your child will be asked to point to the pictures in the order they were previously displayed. The answer will receive 2 points for correctly identifying the pictures in the correct order. If the pictures are correctly identified but not in the correct order, the answer will receive 1 point.

Instructions

Begin children of all ages at exercise one. The pictures your child will need to remember are displayed on the stimulus page. Show your child the stimulus page for about 5 seconds. Then reveal the response pictures on the next page. Do not show your child the stimulus page more than one time. As your child points to the pictures, write a "1" below his first choice, a "2" below his second choice, and so on. Check the answers with the answer key on page 283.

Say:
"This is a memory game. Look at these pictures. Try to remember these pictures and remember the order that they are in."

1

Instructions

Say: **"Point to the pictures that you just saw. Make sure you point to them in the correct order.**

1

A   B   C   D   E   F

Instructions
Say:
"Look at these pictures. Try to remember these pictures and remember the order that they are in."

2

Instructions

Say: **"Point to the pictures that you just saw. Make sure you point to them in the correct order.**

2

A   B   C   D   E   F

Picture Span

Instructions
Say:
"Look at these pictures. Try to remember these pictures and remember the order that they are in."

3

<u>Instructions</u>
Say: **"Point to the pictures that you just saw. Make sure you point to them in the correct order.**

3

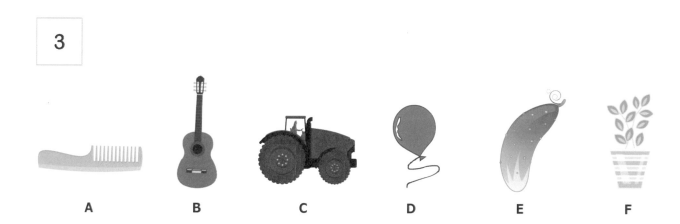

A   B   C   D   E   F

Instructions
Say:
"Look at these pictures. Try to remember these pictures and remember the order that they are in."

4

<u>Instructions</u>
Say: **"Point to the pictures that you just saw. Make sure you point to them in the correct order.**

4

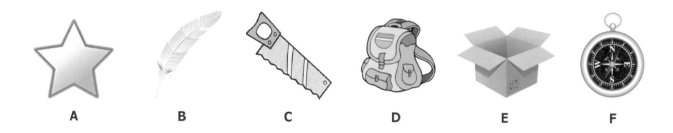

A   B   C   D   E   F

Instructions
Say:
"Look at these pictures. Try to remember these pictures and remember the order that they are in."

5

Instructions

Say: **"Point to the pictures that you just saw. Make sure you point to them in the correct order.**

5

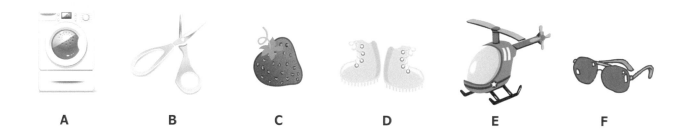

A   B   C   D   E   F

Instructions
Say:
"Look at these pictures. Try to remember these pictures and remember the order that they are in."

6

Instructions
Say: **"Point to the pictures that you just saw. Make sure you point to them in the correct order.**

6

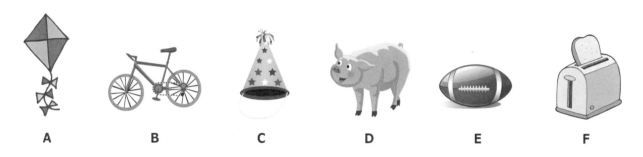

| A | B | C | D | E | F |

Instructions
Say:
"Look at these pictures. Try to remember these pictures and remember the order that they are in."

7

Instructions
Say: **"Point to the pictures that you just saw. Make sure you point to them in the correct order.**

7

| A | B | C | D | E | F |

Instructions

Say:

"Look at these pictures. Try to remember these pictures and remember the order that they are in."

8

Instructions

Say: **"Point to the pictures that you just saw. Make sure you point to them in the correct order.**

8

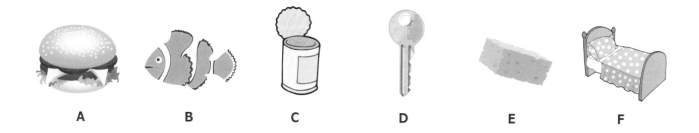

| A | B | C | D | E | F |

Instructions
Say:
"Look at these pictures. Try to remember these pictures and remember the order that they are in."

9

<u>Instructions</u>
Say: **"Point to the pictures that you just saw. Make sure you point to them in the correct order.**

9

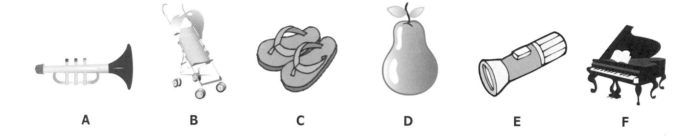

| A | B | C | D | E | F |

Instructions
Say:
"Look at these pictures. Try to remember these pictures and remember the order that they are in."

10

Instructions
Say: "Point to the pictures that you just saw. Make sure you point to them in the correct order.

10

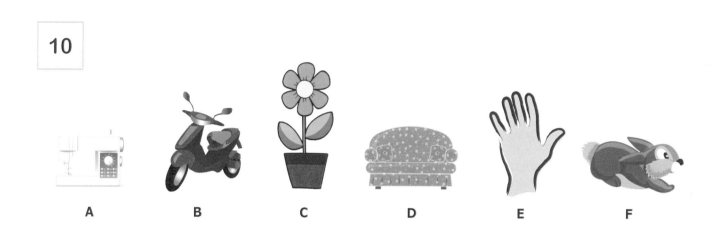

| A | B | C | D | E | F |

Say:
"Look at these pictures. Try to remember these pictures and remember the order that they are in."

11

<u>Instructions</u>
Say: **"Point to the pictures that you just saw. Make sure you point to them in the correct order.**

11

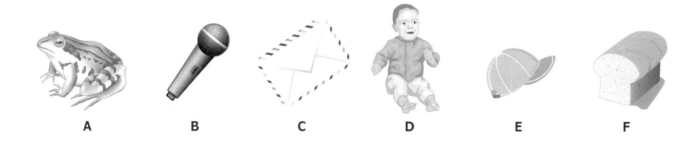

A   B   C   D   E   F

Picture Span

Say:
"Look at these pictures. Try to remember these pictures and remember the order that they are in."

12

<u>Instructions</u>
Say: **"Point to the pictures that you just saw. Make sure you point to them in the correct order.**

12

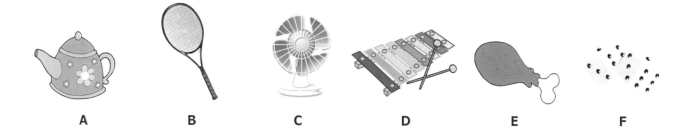

A   B   C   D   E   F

Instructions
Say:
"Look at these pictures. Try to remember these pictures and remember the order that they are in."

13

Instructions
Say: "**Point to the pictures that you just saw. Make sure you point to them in the correct order.**

13

A   B   C   D   E   F

Instructions
Say:
"Look at these pictures. Try to remember these pictures and remember the order that they are in."

14

<u>Instructions</u>
Say: **"Point to the pictures that you just saw. Make sure you point to them in the correct order.**

14

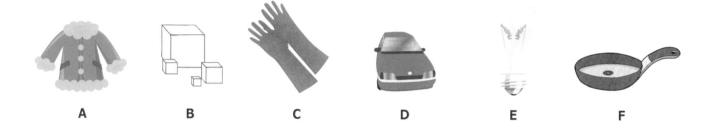

| A | B | C | D | E | F |

<u>Instructions</u>
Say:
"Look at these pictures. Try to remember these pictures and remember the order that they are in."

15

Instructions
Say: "**Point to the pictures that you just saw. Make sure you point to them in the correct order.**

15

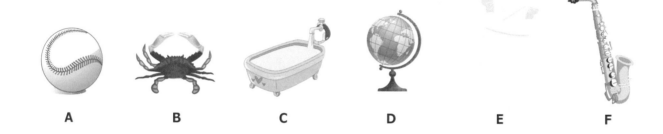

| A | B | C | D | E | F |

Picture Span

Instructions
Say:
"Look at these pictures. Try to remember these pictures and remember the order that they are in."

 16

Instructions
Say: "**Point to the pictures that you just saw. Make sure you point to them in the correct order.**

16

| A | B | C | D | E | F |

Picture Span

Say:
"Look at these pictures. Try to remember these pictures and remember the order that they are in."

17

<u>Instructions</u>
Say: **"Point to the pictures that you just saw. Make sure you point to them in the correct order.**

17

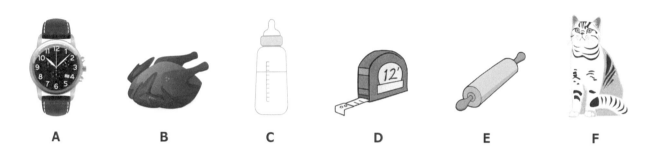

A   B   C   D   E   F

Say:
"Look at these pictures. Try to remember these pictures and remember the order that they are in."

18

Instructions
Say: **"Point to the pictures that you just saw. Make sure you point to them in the correct order.**

18

| A | B | C | D | E | F |

Picture Span

Say:
"Look at these pictures. Try to remember these pictures and remember the order that they are in."

19

Instructions
Say: **"Point to the pictures that you just saw. Make sure you point to them in the correct order.**

19

A   B   C   D   E   F

Instructions
Say:
"Look at these pictures. Try to remember these pictures and remember the order that they are in."

20

Instructions
Say: **"Point to the pictures that you just saw. Make sure you point to them in the correct order.**

20

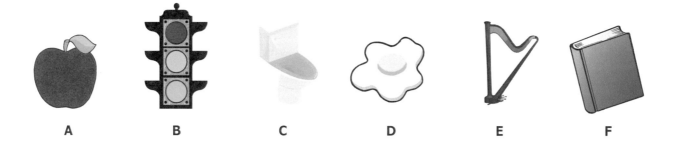

A   B   C   D   E   F

Say:
"Look at these pictures. Try to remember these pictures and remember the order that they are in."

21

Instructions
Say: **"Point to the pictures that you just saw. Make sure you point to them in the correct order.**

21

| A | B | C | D | E | F |

Say:

"Look at these pictures. Try to remember these pictures and remember the order that they are in."

22

Instructions
Say: "**Point to the pictures that you just saw. Make sure you point to them in the correct order.**"

22

| A | B | C | D | E | F |

Picture Span

Instructions
Say:
"Look at these pictures. Try to remember these pictures and remember the order that they are in."

23

Instructions

Say: **"Point to the pictures that you just saw. Make sure you point to them in the correct order.**

23

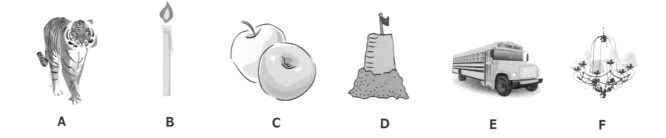

A   B   C   D   E   F

Instructions
Say:
"Look at these pictures. Try to remember these pictures and remember the order that they are in."

24

Instructions
Say: **"Point to the pictures that you just saw. Make sure you point to them in the correct order.**

24

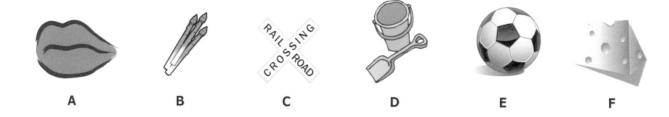

A   B   C   D   E   F

Instructions

Say:
"Look at these pictures. Try to remember these pictures and remember the order that they are in."

25

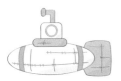

Instructions
Say: "Point to the pictures that you just saw. Make sure you point to them in the correct order.

25

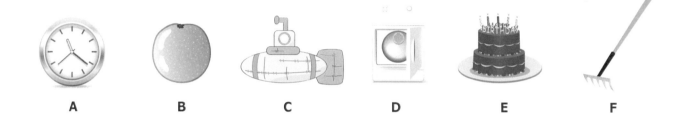

| A | B | C | D | E | F |

Instructions
Say:
"Look at these pictures. Try to remember these pictures and remember the order that they are in."

 26

Instructions

Say: **"Point to the pictures that you just saw. Make sure you point to them in the correct order.**

26

A   B   C   D   E   F

Instructions
Say:
"Look at these pictures. Try to remember these pictures and remember the order that they are in."

27

Instructions
Say: **"Point to the pictures that you just saw. Make sure you point to them in the correct order.**

27

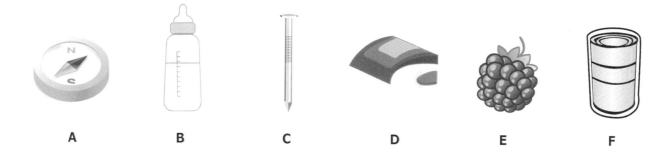

| A | B | C | D | E | F |

Picture Span

Say:
"**Look at these pictures. Try to remember these pictures and remember the order that they are in.**"

28

<u>Instructions</u>
Say: **"Point to the pictures that you just saw. Make sure you point to them in the correct order.**

28

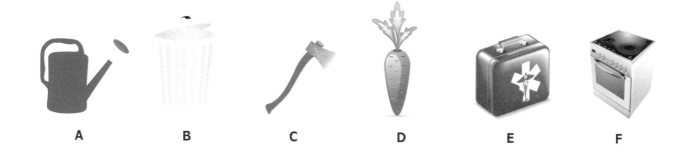

| A | B | C | D | E | F |

Picture Span

Say:
"Look at these pictures. Try to remember these pictures and remember the order that they are in."

29

Instructions
Say: "Point to the pictures that you just saw. Make sure you point to them in the correct order.

29

| A | B | C | D | E | F |

Instructions
Say:
"Look at these pictures. Try to remember these pictures and remember the order that they are in."

30

Instructions
Say: "**Point to the pictures that you just saw. Make sure you point to them in the correct order.**

30

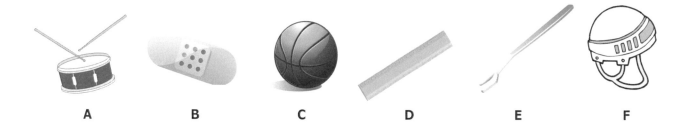

A   B   C   D   E   F

Instructions
Say:
"Look at these pictures. Try to remember these pictures and remember the order that they are in."

31

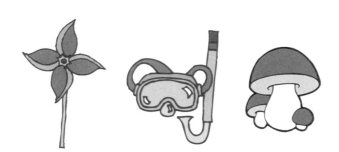

Instructions
Say: "Point to the pictures that you just saw. Make sure you point to them in the correct order.

31

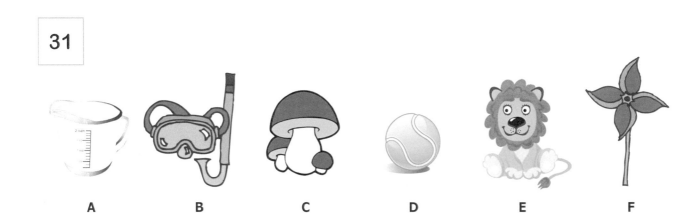

| A | B | C | D | E | F |

Instructions

Say:

"Look at these pictures. Try to remember these pictures and remember the order that they are in."

32

Instructions
Say: **"Point to the pictures that you just saw. Make sure you point to them in the correct order.**

32

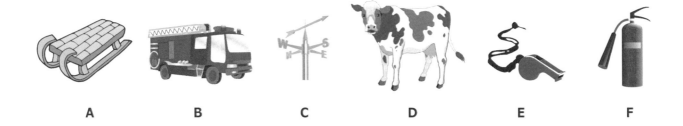

A   B   C   D   E   F

Picture Span

Say:
"Look at these pictures. Try to remember these pictures and remember the order that they are in."

33

Instructions
Say: "**Point to the pictures that you just saw. Make sure you point to them in the correct order.**

33

| A | B | C | D | E | F |

Picture Span

Say:
"**Look at these pictures. Try to remember these pictures and remember the order that they are in.**"

34

Say: **"Point to the pictures that you just saw. Make sure you point to them in the correct order.**

34

| A | B | C | D | E | F |

Picture Span

Instructions
Say:
"Look at these pictures. Try to remember these pictures and remember the order that they are in."

35

Say: "**Point to the pictures that you just saw. Make sure you point to them in the correct order.**

35

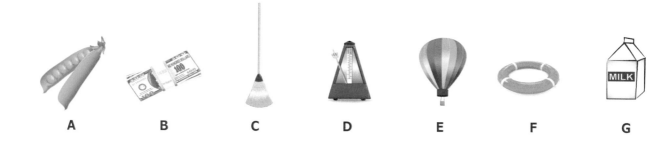

A   B   C   D   E   F   G

Picture Span

Say:
"**Look at these pictures. Try to remember these pictures and remember the order that they are in.**"

36

Instructions

Say: **"Point to the pictures that you just saw. Make sure you point to them in the correct order.**

36

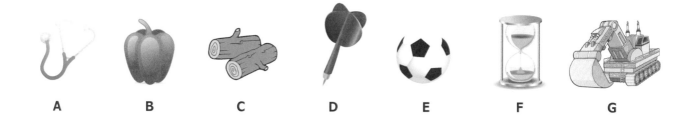

A   B   C   D   E   F   G

Picture Span

Instructions
Say:
"**Look at these pictures. Try to remember these pictures and remember the order that they are in.**"

37

Instructions

Say: **"Point to the pictures that you just saw. Make sure you point to them in the correct order.**

37

| A | B | C | D | E | F | G |

Instructions
Say:
"Look at these pictures. Try to remember these pictures and remember the order that they are in."

38

276

Instructions

Say: **"Point to the pictures that you just saw. Make sure you point to them in the correct order.**

38

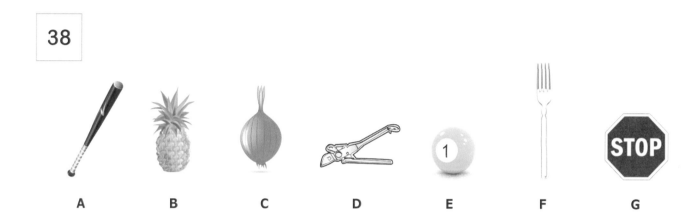

| A | B | C | D | E | F | G |

Instructions

Say:

"Look at these pictures. Try to remember these pictures and remember the order that they are in."

39

Instructions
Say: "**Point to the pictures that you just saw. Make sure you point to them in the correct order.**

39

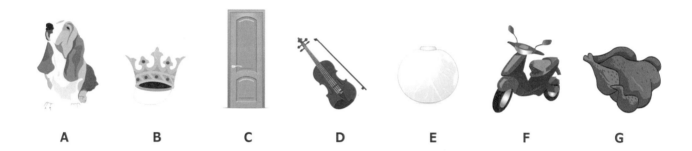

| A | B | C | D | E | F | G |

Instructions
Say:
"Look at these pictures. Try to remember these pictures and remember the order that they are in."

40

<u>Instructions</u>
Say: **"Point to the pictures that you just saw. Make sure you point to them in the correct order.**

40

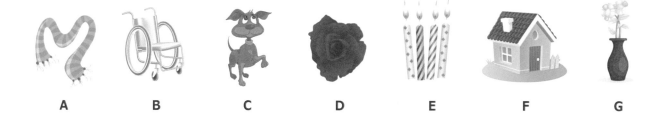

| A | B | C | D | E | F | G |

Instructions

Say:

"Look at these pictures. Try to remember these pictures and remember the order that they are in."

41

Say: **"Point to the pictures that you just saw. Make sure you point to them in the correct order.**

41

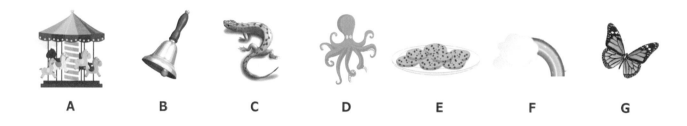

| A | B | C | D | E | F | G |

Answer Key

1. E, F	26. A, D, C
2. B, C	27. B, C, A
3. C, E	28. B, D, E
4. C, F	29. B, C, D
5. B, E	30. F, A, D
6. A, E	31. F, B, C
7. A, D	32. B, D, A
8. D, B	33. F, D, C
9. D, C	34. C, A, E
10. E, B	35. B, D, F, G
11. D, A, F	36. A, F, C, E
12. D, B, E	37. B, A, D, F
13. C, A, D	38. B, D, A, C
14. E, C, B	39. A, C, F, E
15. F, D, B	40. C, E, F, G
16. F, B, A	41. B, E, C, F
17. A, F, D	
18. A, E, B	
19. D, C, F	
20. F, A, B	
21. D, B, E	
22. D, E, C	
23. A, E, B	
24. E, F, D	
25. C, A, E	

Description

Using a key, the child draws symbols that are paired with objects. Each correct answer receives 1 point. The score is based on the number of correctly drawn symbols within a 120–second time limit.

Materials

- Coding Worksheets A or B
- 1 pencil
- Clock or Stopwatch

Instructions

There are 2 types of coding worksheets. Worksheet A is for children ages 6-7. Worksheet B is for children ages 8-16. Please use the worksheet appropriate for your child. Ask your child to do one worksheet a day.

Coding Worksheet A

Instructions

Place the first coding worksheet on a table or desk in front of your child. Give him/her a pencil and pointing to the key say:

"**Look at these objects** (point to the key). **Do you see how the flower has a line going down the middle?**"

"**Now look at these objects without any marks in them** (point to objects below the key line). **I want you to write the same marks that are up here** (point to the key) **in these objects down here** (point to the objects below the key line)."

"**Let me show you. Here is the flower** (point to bottom objects). **Look up at the top to find the flower** (point to key). **See how the flower has a line going down the middle** (point to the line)? **I need you to draw a line in the middle of this flower like this** (draw a line in the flower)."

"**Let me show you again. Here is the leaf** (point to bottom objects). **Look up at the top to find the leaf** (point to key). **See how the leaf has a line going across the middle** (point to the line)? **I need you to draw a line in the middle of this leaf like this** (draw a line in the leaf)."

"**Now I want you to give it a try. Mark all the objects on the page without skipping any of them. When I say 'go' I want you to begin. OK?**"

"**Are you ready?...Go.**" Begin timing your child. The primary goal is a help your child correctly complete one page within 120 seconds. Record the completion time at the bottom of each worksheet page. Check responses with the answer keys beginning on page 289.

Exercise 1

   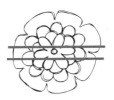

Time (Max. 120 seconds)   Total Correct   % Correct

_____   _____   /62 x 100= _____

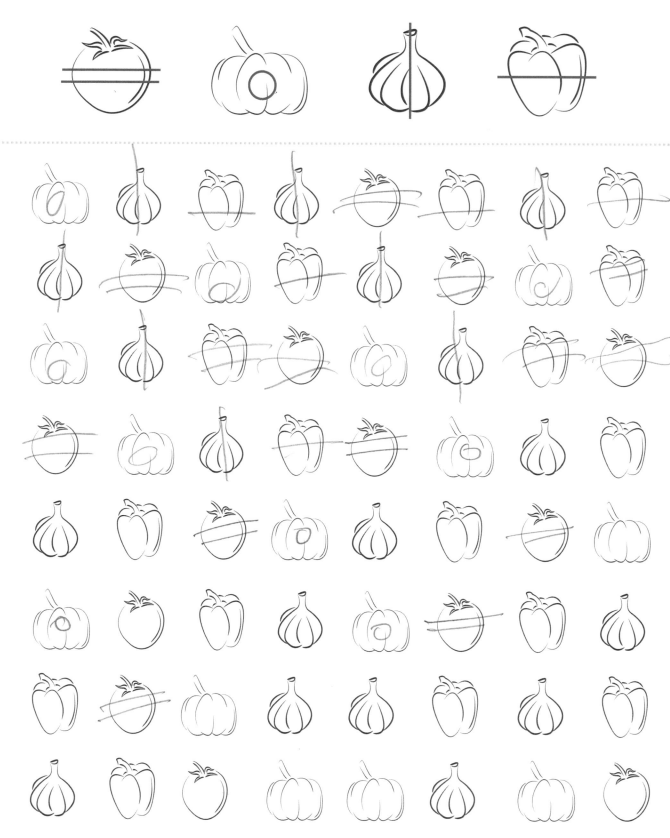

Time (Max. 120 seconds)　　　　Total Correct　　　　% Correct

/64 x 100=

   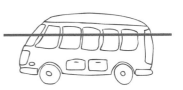

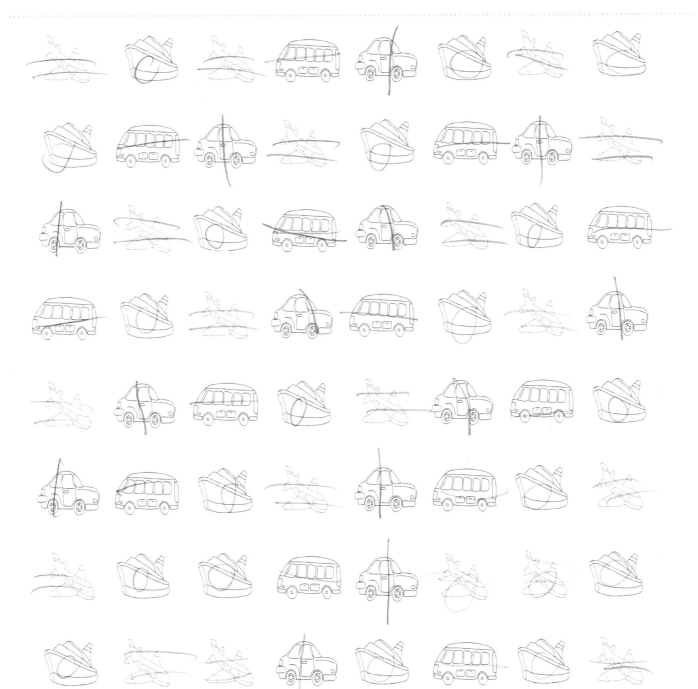

Time (Max. 120 seconds)   Total Correct   % Correct

                                                        /64 x 100=

Exercise 4

 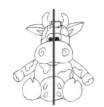  

Time (Max. 120 seconds)   Total Correct   % Correct

/64 x 100=

Coding A

   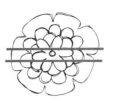

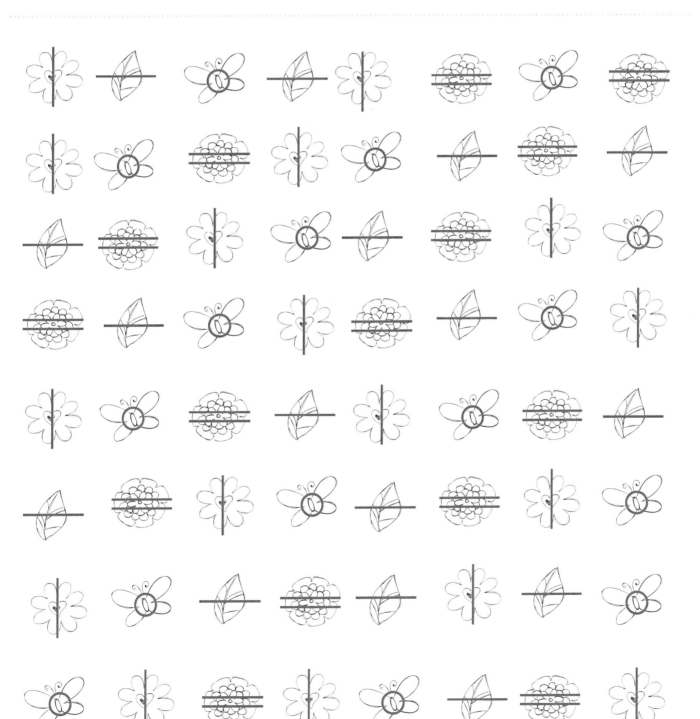

   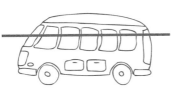

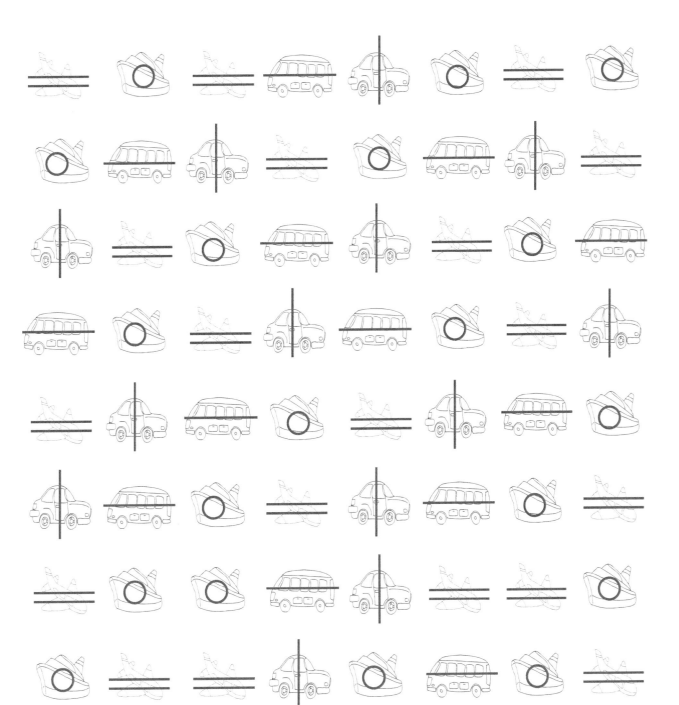

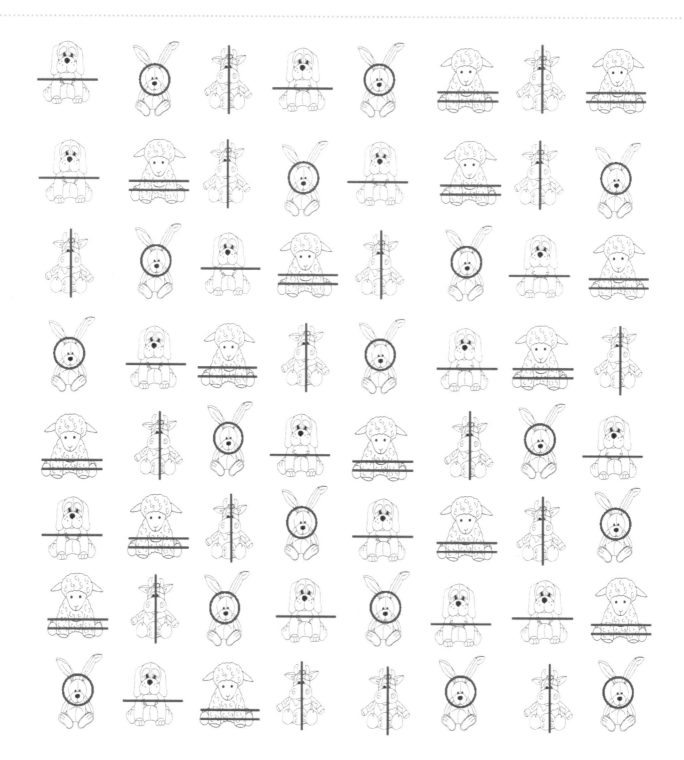

Coding Worksheet B

Instructions
Place coding worksheet B (beginning on page 294) on a table or desk in front of your child. Give him/her a pencil and pointing to the key say:

"**Look at these boxes** (point to the key). **Each box has a letter at the top** (move your finger along the letters from A to I) **and a mark at the bottom** (move your finger along the symbols). **Each letter has its own mark."**

Point to the practice items and say: "**Here the boxes have letters at the top but nothing in the bottom part. I want you to draw the marks that go in the empty boxes."**

"**Let me show you. Here is a D** (point to the D in the practice items). **The D's mark is this circle with a dot in the middle** (point to the symbol). **So I will draw this mark in the empty box, watch me** (draw the symbol)."

"**I'll show you again. Here is a B** (point to B in the practice items). **The B's mark is a triangle** (point to the symbol). **So I will draw a triangle in the empty box, like this** (draw the triangle)."

Give your child a pencil and say: "**Now you do the rest. Go in order and don't skip any. Stop when you get to the end of the page** (point to the end of the page)."

"**Are you ready?...Go."** Start timing your child. Record the completion time and total number of correct answers in the space provided at the bottom of the page. The answer key can be found on page 298.

To get a perfect score, your child must complete all of the exercises correctly within 120 seconds. Let your child practice one exercise page each day until he/she has mastered the task.

Exercise 1

KEY

A	B	C	D	E	F	G	H	I
○	△	Ɔ	⊙	=	⊥	:	>	⊖

Practice Items:

D	B

C	E	D	I	A	F	H	E	D	I	B	A	H	B	E	D	F	I	A	C
Ɔ	=	⊙	⊖	○	⊥	>	=	⊙	⊖	△	○	>	△	=	⊙	⊥	⊖	○	Ɔ

A	G	B	I	C	D	E	D	C	H	A	F	E	G	I	A	H	F	I	D

B	F	A	H	B	I	D	G	F	E	A	B	H	G	C	E	H	D	A	E

D	I	G	E	H	A	F	D	E	H	G	I	A	B	C	I	E	B	C	D

F	A	I	E	G	F	C	H	I	G	B	F	D	E	A	I	G	E	B	H

I	B	G	E	A	D	E	I	G	B	C	F	A	H	G	D	I	A	B	F

Time (Max. 120 sec.)   Total Correct   % Correct

_____   _____   /120 x 100= _____

A	B	C	D	E	F	G	H	I
□	◁	↓	?	#	←	0	=	X

G	F	E	B	A	C	H	I	D	G	B	H	D	A	C	I	B	F	C	F

B	D	H	E	A	C	D	I	H	E	F	I	C	A	B	I	G	E	C	B

H	B	E	C	H	A	I	H	D	B	F	A	C	E	H	B	A	I	G	C

C	I	A	D	H	B	E	G	C	B	E	A	I	B	F	C	E	D	G	A

G	H	E	I	C	B	E	I	F	A	C	E	H	C	G	H	A	E	F	H

A	B	G	C	B	E	I	F	H	A	G	C	I	F	D	B	H	A	E	G

Time (Max. 120 sec.)   Total Correct   % Correct

/120 x 100=

A	B	C	D	E	F	G	H	I
?	>	—	⊙	<	:	=	⊖	△

C	E	D	I	A	F	H	E	D	I	B	A	H	B	E	D	F	I	A	C

A	G	B	I	C	D	E	D	C	H	A	F	E	G	I	A	H	F	I	D

B	F	A	H	B	I	D	G	F	E	A	B	H	G	C	E	H	D	A	E

D	I	G	E	H	A	F	D	E	H	G	I	A	B	C	I	E	B	C	D

F	A	I	E	G	F	C	H	I	G	B	F	D	E	A	I	G	E	B	H

I	B	G	E	A	D	E	I	G	B	C	F	A	H	G	D	I	A	B	F

Time (Max. 120 sec.)   Total Correct   % Correct

_____   _____   /120 x 100= _____

Coding B

A	B	C	D	E	F	G	H	I
>	X	⊥	]	⊖	<	:	[	?

G	F	E	B	A	C	H	I	D	G	B	H	D	A	C	I	B	F	C	F

B	D	H	E	A	C	D	I	H		F	I	C	A	B	I	G	E	C	B

H	B	E	C	H	A	I	H	D	B	F	A	C	E	H	B	A	I	G	C

C	I	A	D	H	B	E	G	C	B	E	A	I	B	F	C	E	D	G	A

G	H	E	I	C	B	E	I	F	A	C	E	H	C	G	H	A	E	F	H

A	B	G	C	B	E	I	F	H	A	G	C	I	F	D	B	H	A	E	G

Time (Max. 120 sec.)   Total Correct   % Correct

/120 x 100=

_____   _____   _____

C	E	D	I	A	F	H	E	D	I	B	A	H	B	E	D	F	I	A	C
Ə	=	⊙	⊖	○	⊥	>	=	⊙	⊖	△	○	>	△	=	⊙	⊥	⊖	○	Ə

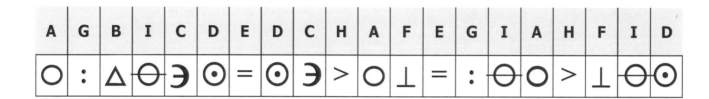

A	G	B	I	C	D	E	D	C	H	A	F	E	G	I	A	H	F	I	D
○	:	△	⊖	Ə	⊙	=	⊙	Ə	>	○	⊥	=	:	⊖	○	>	⊥	⊖	⊙

B	F	A	H	B	I	D	G	F	E	A	B	H	G	C	E	H	D	A	E
△	⊥	○	>	△	⊖	⊙	:	⊥	=	○	△	>	:	Ə	=	>	⊙	○	=

D	I	G	E	H	A	F	D	E	H	G	I	A	B	C	I	E	B	C	D
⊙	⊖	:	=	>	○	⊥	⊙	=	>	:	⊖	○	△	Ə	⊖	=	△	Ə	⊙

F	A	I	E	G	F	C	H	I	G	B	F	D	E	A	I	G	E	B	H
⊥	○	⊖	=	:	⊥	Ə	>	⊖	:	△	⊥	⊙	=	○	⊖	:	=	△	>

I	B	G	E	A	D	E	I	G	B	C	F	A	H	G	D	I	A	B	F
⊖	△	:	=	○	○	⊙	=	⊖	:	△	Ə	⊥	○	>	:	⊙	⊖	○	△	⊥

G	F	E	B	A	C	H	I	D	G	B	H	D	A	C	I	B	F	C	F
0	←	#	◁	□	↓	=	x	?	0	◁	=	?	□	↓	x	◁	←	↓	←

B	D	H	E	A	C	D	I	H	E	F	I	C	A	B	I	G	E	C	B
◁	?	=	#	□	↓	?	x	=	#	←	x	↓	□	◁	x	0	#	↓	◁

H	B	E	C	H	A	I	H	D	B	F	A	C	E	H	B	A	I	G	C
=	◁	#	↓	=	□	x	=	?	◁	←	□	↓	#	=	◁	□	x	0	↓

C	I	A	D	H	B	E	G	C	B	E	A	I	B	F	C	E	D	G	A
↓	x	□	?	=	◁	#	0	↓	◁	#	□	x	◁	←	↓	#	?	0	□

G	H	E	I	C	B	E	I	F	A	C	E	H	C	G	H	A	E	F	H
0	=	#	x	↓	◁	#	x	←	□	↓	#	=	↓	0	=	□	#	←	=

A	B	G	C	B	E	I	F	H	A	G	C	I	F	D	B	H	A	E	G
□	◁	0	↓	◁	#	x	←	=	□	0	↓	x	←	?	◁	=	□	#	0

C	E	D	I	A	F	H	E	D	I	B	A	H	B	E	D	F	I	A	C
−	<	⊙	△	?	:	⊖	<	⊙	△	>	?	⊖	>	<	⊙	:	△	?	−

A	G	B	I	C	D	E	D	C	H	A	F	E	G	I	A	H	F	I	D
?	=	>	△	−	⊙	<	⊙	−	⊖	?	:	<	=	△	?	⊖	:	△	⊙

B	F	A	H	B	I	D	G	F	E	A	B	H	G	C	E	H	D	A	E
>	:	?	⊖	>	△	⊙	=	:	<	?	>	⊖	=	−	<	⊖	⊙	?	<

D	I	G	E	H	A	F	D	E	H	G	I	A	B	C	I	E	B	C	D
⊙	△	=	<	⊖	?	:	⊙	<	⊖	=	△	?	>	−	△	<	>	−	⊙

F	A	I	E	G	F	C	H	I	G	B	F	D	E	A	I	G	E	B	H
:	?	△	<	=	:	−	⊖	△	=	>	:	⊙	<	?	△	=	<	>	⊖

I	B	G	E	A	D	E	I	G	B	C	F	A	H	G	D	I	A	B	F
△	>	=	<	?	⊙	<	△	=	>	−	:	?	⊖	=	⊙	△	?	>	:

G	F	E	B	A	C	H	I	D	G	B	H	D	A	C	I	B	F	C	F
:	<	⊖	X	>	⊥	[	?	]	:	X	[	]	>	⊥	?	X	<	⊥	<

B	D	H	E	A	C	D	I	H	G	F	I	C	A	B	I	G	E	C	B
X	]	[	⊖	>	⊥	]	?	[	:	<	?	⊥	>	X	?	:	⊖	⊥	X

H	B	E	C	H	A	I	H	D	B	F	A	C	E	H	B	A	I	G	C
[	X	⊖	⊥	[	>	?	[	]	X	<	>	⊥	⊖	[	X	>	?	:	⊥

C	I	A	D	H	B	E	G	C	B	E	A	I	B	F	C	E	D	G	A
⊥	?	>	]	[	X	⊖	:	⊥	X	⊖	>	?	X	<	⊥	⊖	]	:	>

G	H	E	I	C	B	E	I	F	A	C	E	H	C	G	H	A	E	F	H
:	[	⊖	?	⊥	X	⊖	?	<	>	⊥	⊖	[	⊥	:	[	>	⊖	<	[

A	B	G	C	B	E	I	F	H	A	G	C	I	F	D	B	H	A	E	G
>	X	:	⊥	X	⊖	?	<	[	>	:	⊥	?	<	]	X	[	>	⊖	:

302

Description

The child, after looking at a target picture and a group of pictures, indicates whether or not the target picture appears in the group of pictures. The child's response is indicated by circling the Y (yes) or N (no). The score is based on the number of correct responses given within a 120-second time limit.

Materials

- Symbol Search Worksheet
- 1 pencil
- Clock or Stopwatch

Instructions

There are two types of symbol search worksheets. Worksheet A is for children ages 6-7. Worksheet B is for children ages 8-16. Please use the worksheet appropriate for your child.

Symbol Search A

Instructions

Place the Symbol Search Worksheet in front of the child. Point to Symbol Search Practice #1, moving your finger from left to right and say: **"Look at these pictures."**

Point to the target picture (Lion) on the far left and say:

> **"This picture is in this group of pictures over here** (point to the pictures in the search group)."

Then, point to the target picture again and say:

> **"Look, this picture here is the same as this picture over here** (point to the matching picture in the search group). **So I will circle 'Y' for yes like this** (Draw a circle around the Y)."

Now, point to Symbol Search Practice #2 and say: **"Now look at these pictures."**

Point to the target picture (cucumber) on the far left and say:

> **"This picture** (point to the cucumber) **is not in this group over here** (point to the search group). **So now I will draw a circle around the 'N' for no** (draw a circle around the N)."

> **"I want you to circle the 'N' if the picture over here** (point to the target picture) **is not the same as any of these pictures** (point to the search group)."

Now, point to the Symbol Search Exercises on page 304 and say:

> **"Now, I want you to do these all by yourself. Do as many as you can as quickly as you can without making mistakes. Please go in order. When I say 'Go' I want you to start. OK?"**
> **"Get ready. Go"**

Time for 120 seconds. Write the completion time on page 306. Check the responses with the answer key beginning on page 307.

Practice Exercises

					Y	N
1					Y	N
2					Y	N

⑧	❺	⑨	⑧	Y	N
✂	✂	✏	🖌	Y	N
🫐	🍎	🍓	🫐	Y	N
🍋	🍑	🍋	🍐	Y	N
🥕	🍆	🫑	🥕	Y	N
🍞	🍞	🍞	🍞	Y	N
↕	↰	✛	⌐	Y	N
☾	⚡	★	↑	Y	N
⊗	◇	⊗	✕	Y	N
▲	◣	▼	▲	Y	N
★	☆	☆	☆	Y	N
▲	●	▲	■	Y	N
●	■	●	▲	Y	N
■	●	▲	■	Y	N
●	●	●	●	Y	N

◈	◈	◈	⊞	Y	N
◎	⊕	◎	◉	Y	N
❧	✿	✹	꩜	Y	N
◠	◰	◠	⚲	Y	N
▲▼▲	◆◆◆	⇒»	▲▼▲	Y	N
★	✺	★	✴	Y	N
✸	▣	◖	◆	Y	N
◷	⊘	◕	⏻	Y	N
✿	🌍	☀	✿	Y	N
⦿	💡	◉	♥	Y	N
⊕	⊖	⚲	⊕	Y	N
⚜	⚜	⚜	⚜	Y	N
🦋	🦋	🦋	🦋	Y	N
🐎	🐘	🐫	🐎	Y	N
🐈	🐇	🐇	🐇	Y	N

				Y	N
☆	✦	💥	☆	Y	N
◎	⌒	⊘	◎	Y	N
☺	✺	☺	○	Y	N
✚	♡	☆	✳	Y	N
⬇	⬅	➡	⬆	Y	N
↶	↷	⤵	⤴	Y	N
○	□	△	○	Y	N
◇	▱	◇	⬡	Y	N
⎆	⎇	⚑	▱	Y	N
⊏	⊐	⬡	⊏	Y	N
☀	☀	✷	✸	Y	N
✚	✚	⇧	✚	Y	N
⬛	▯	▫	▭	Y	N
⬚	▯	▯	⬚	Y	N
▱	▱	▱	▱	Y	N

Time (Max. 120 sec.)   Total Correct   % Correct

_____   _____   _____

/45 x 100 =

Answer Key

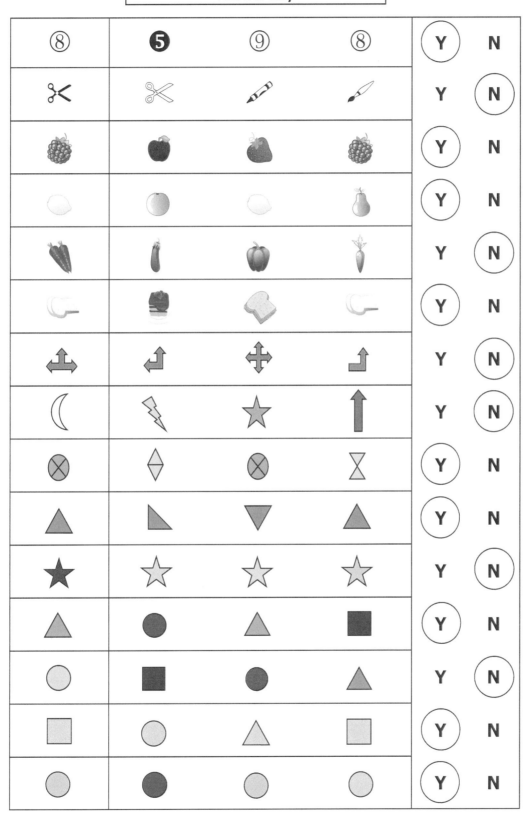

Answer Key					
◆	◆◆	◬	✪✪	Y	**(N)**
◉	⊕	◎	▣	**(Y)**	N
✤	✺	✷	🐚	Y	**(N)**
◖	∟	👁	⚕	Y	**(N)**
▲▼▲	◆》	⇛	▲▼▲	**(Y)**	N
★	✺	★	✴	**(Y)**	N
✼	☀	☯	◆	Y	**(N)**
🕐	🚫	🥧	⏻	Y	**(N)**
✾	🌍	☀	✾	**(Y)**	N
📡	💡	⛟	♥	Y	**(N)**
⊕	⊖	⚲	⊕	**(Y)**	N
⚜	⚜	⚜	⚜	**(Y)**	N
🦋	🦋	🦋	🦋	**(Y)**	N
🐎	🐘	🐫	🐎	**(Y)**	N
🐈	🐰	🐰	🐕	Y	**(N)**

		Answer Key			

				Y / N
☆	✦	💥	☆	**Y** / N
◎	⌒	🚫	◎	**Y** / N
☺	☀	☺	○	**Y** / N
✛	♡	☆	✦	Y / **N**
⬇	⬅	➡	⬆	Y / **N**
↺	↻	⤵	⤴	Y / **N**
○	□	△	○	**Y** / N
◇	▱	◇	⬡	**Y** / N
⟁	⟁	▱	⟁	Y / **N**
▭	◗	⬡	▭	**Y** / N
☀	☀	✸	✸	**Y** / N
✚	✚	⛉	✚	**Y** / N
⬛	▯	▪	⬛	Y / **N**
⬤	▮	▮	⬤	Y / **N**
▱	▱	◢	▱	**Y** / N

SYMBOL SEARCH B

Instructions

Place the Symbol Search Worksheet B in front of your child. Point to Symbol Search Practice #1, moving your finger from left to right and say: **"Look at these pictures."**

Point to the target pictures (lion & teddy) on the far left and say:

> **"One of these pictures is in this group of pictures over here** (point to the pictures in the search group).**"**

Then, point to the target pictures again and say:

> **"Look, this picture here is the same as this picture over here** (point to the matching picture in the search group). **So I will circle 'Y' for yes like this** (draw a circle around the Y).**"**

Now, point to Symbol Search Practice #2 and say: **"Now look at these pictures."**

Point to the target pictures (cucumber & melon) on the far left and say:

> **"Neither of these pictures** (point to the cucumber & melon) **is in this group over here** (point to the search group). **So now I will draw a circle around the 'N' for no** (draw a circle around the N).**"**

> "**I want you to circle the 'N' if the picture over here** (point to the target picture) **is not the same as any of these pictures** (point to the search group).**"**

Now, point to the Symbol Search Exercises on the next page and say:

> **"Now, I want you to do these all by yourself. Do as many as you can as quickly as you can without making mistakes. Please go in order. When I say 'Go' I want you to start. OK?"**
> **"Get ready. Go"**

Time for 120 seconds. Write the completion time on page 315. Check the responses with the answer key beginning on page 316.

Practice Exercises

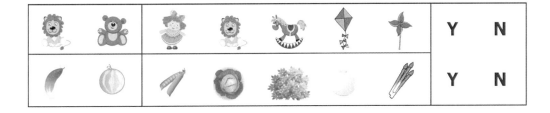

1								Y	N
2								Y	N

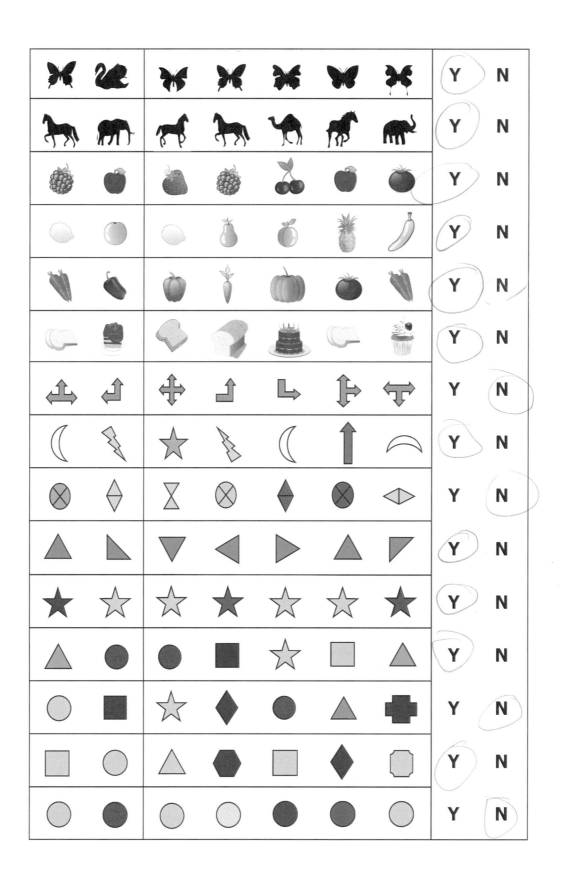

Symbol Search B

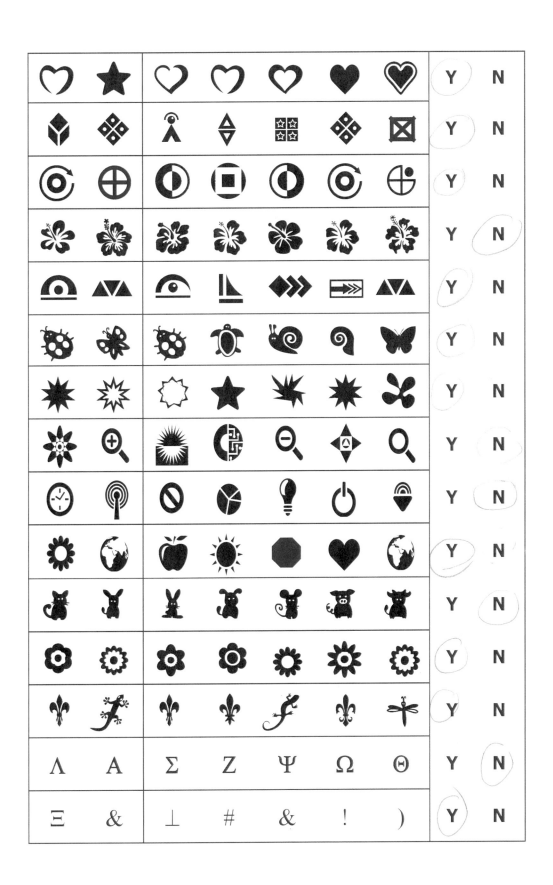

Target		Search Group					Response	
♡	★	♡	♡	♡	♥	♥	(Y)	N
◈	❖	⚐	◮	⊞	◈	⊠	(Y)	N
◉	⊕	◐	▣	◑	◉	⊕	(Y)	N
❀	❁	❁	❀	❃	❋	❀	Y	(N)
◓	▲▽	◉	⌐	◆▶	⇒	▲▽	(Y)	N
🐞	🦋	🐞	🐢	🐌	@	🦋	(Y)	N
✴	✸	✹	★	✷	✴	✿	Y	N
✺	🔍	☀	⊚	⊖	◈	🔍	Y	(N)
🕐	📡	🚫	◕	💡	⏻	◓	Y	(N)
✿	🌍	🍎	☀	⬢	♥	🌍	(Y)	N
🐱	🐰	🐰	🐭	🐭	🐷	🐱	Y	(N)
✿	❁	✿	❀	❋	✺	❁	(Y)	N
⚜	🦎	⚜	⚜	🦎	⚜	🦟	(Y)	N
Λ	A	Σ	Z	Ψ	Ω	Θ	Y	(N)
Ξ	&	⊥	#	&	!	)	(Y)	N

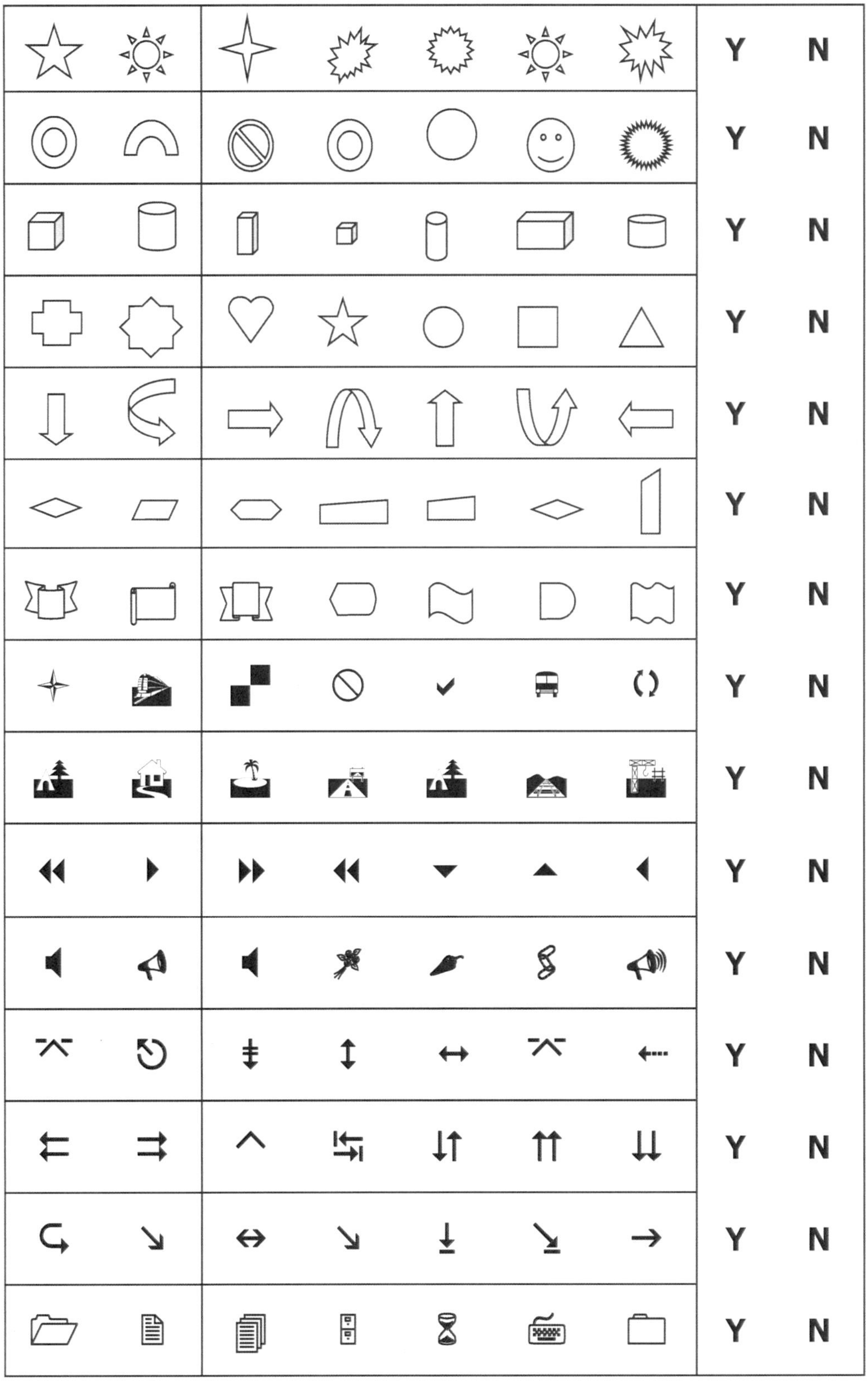
Y N
Y N
Y N
Y N
Y N
Y N
Y N
Y N
Y N
Y N
Y N
Y N
Y N
Y N
Y N

							Y	N
							Y	N
							Y	N
							Y	N
							Y	N
							Y	N
							Y	N
							Y	N
							Y	N
							Y	N
							Y	N
							Y	N
							Y	N
							Y	N
							Y	N

Time (Max. 120 sec.)   Total Correct   % Correct

/60 x 100 =

Answer Key

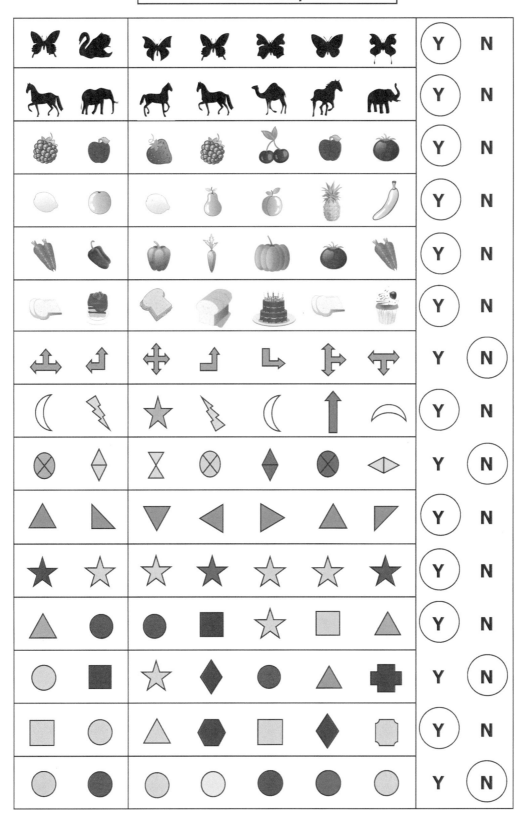

							Answer
♡	★	♡	♡	♡	♥	♥	**Y** / N
◆	❖		◬		❖	⊠	**Y** / N
◉	⊕	◐	⊡	◑	◉	⊕	**Y** / N
❀	❀	❀	❀	❀	❀	❀	Y / **N**
	◭						**Y** / N
			🐢	🐌		🦋	**Y** / N
✹	✸		★		✹		**Y** / N
✿	⊕			⊖	◈	⚲	Y / **N**
⊙					⏻		Y / **N**
✿	🌍	🍎	☀	⬡	♥	🌍	**Y** / N
🐱		🐰	🐭	🐭	🐷		Y / **N**
❁	❁	❁	❁	❁	❁	❁	**Y** / N
⚜	🦎	⚜	⚜	🦎	⚜		**Y** / N
Λ	A	Σ	Z	Ψ	Ω	Θ	Y / **N**
Ξ	&	⊥	#	&	!	)	**Y** / N

☆	☼	✦	✺	✺	☀	✸	**Y**	N
◎	⌒	🚫	◎	○	☺	✺	**Y**	N
⬡	⬭	▯	▫	▮	▱	⬭	Y	**N**
✚	✺	♡	☆	○	□	△	Y	**N**
⬇	↪	⇒	⋂	⬆	⤴	⬅	Y	**N**
◇	▱	⬡	▭	▭	◇	▯	**Y**	N
🏴	🏳	🏴	⬡	〰	🏳	⬡	Y	**N**
✦	🏞	◼	🚫	✔	🚌	()	Y	**N**
🏔	🏠	🏝	🏞	🏔	🏟	🏗	**Y**	N
⏪	▶	⏩	⏪	▼	▲	◀	**Y**	N
🔈	📢	🔈	🎇	🌶	🐛	🔊	**Y**	N
⋋	↺	⇳	↕	↔	⋋	⇠	**Y**	N
⇇	⇉	⋀	⇄	⇅	⇈	⇊	Y	**N**
↰	↘	↔	↘	↓	↘	→	**Y**	N
🗁	📄	🗐	▤	⧖	⌨	🗀	Y	**N**

				Answer Key				

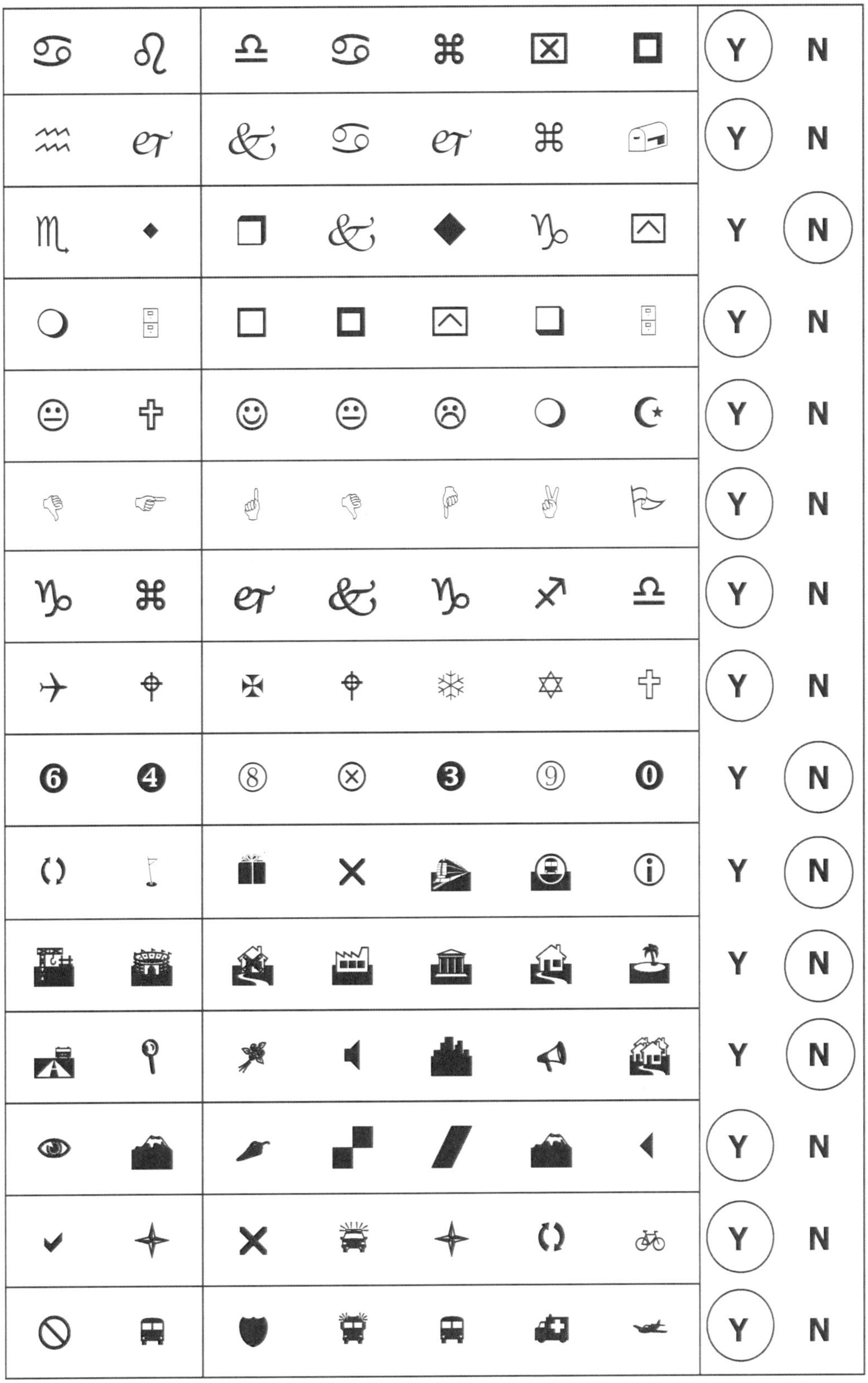

This page is a symbol search worksheet. Each row contains two target symbols, five comparison symbols, and Y/N answer circles.

Targets	Comparison Symbols	Answer
♋ ♌	♎ ♋ ⌘ ⊠ ■	**Y** N
♒ ℰ	& ♋ ℰ ⌘ 📫	**Y** N
♏ ◆	□ & ◆ ♑ ⌂	Y **N**
◐ ▯	□ ■ ⌂ ▢ ▯	**Y** N
😐 ✝	☺ 😐 ☹ ◐ ☪	**Y** N
👎 ☞	☝ 👎 👇 ✌ ⚑	**Y** N
♑ ⌘	ℰ & ♑ ♐ ♎	**Y** N
✈ ☠	✠ ☧ ❄ ✡ ✝	**Y** N
❻ ❹	⑧ ⊗ ❸ ⑨ ⓪	Y **N**
⟨⟩ ⚑	🎁 ✕ ✉ ⊜ ⓘ	Y **N**
🏭 🏰	🏚 🏭 🏛 🏠 🏝	Y **N**
🏕 ♀	💐 ◀ 🏢 📢 🏘	Y **N**
👁 🏔	🌶 ▰ ╱ 🏔 ◀	**Y** N
✔ ✦	✕ 🚨 ✦ ⟨⟩ 🚲	**Y** N
🚫 🚌	🛡 🚌 🚌 🚑 ✈	**Y** N

Description:

The cancellation subtest is comprised of 2 parts. During the first part your child will be asked to mark specific pictures shown among a random group of other pictures within a time limit of 45 seconds. During the second part, your child will be asked to mark specific pictures shown among a group of objects in linear order. The score is based on the total incorrect responses subtracted from the total correct responses. Bonus points will be awarded if the subtest is completed in less than 45 seconds.

Materials:

- Pencil
- Stopwatch or Clock

Practice Instructions:

Use the example on the next page to explain this subtest to your child. Begin by pointing to the first row of pictures below and saying: **"Look at these pictures. They are all pictures of food. Now look at these pictures below the line** (point to the pictures below the line). **They are pictures of food and other things. I will draw a line across each picture of food like this** (draw lines across each picture of food)."

Exercise Instructions:

Say: **"Now I want you to do the same thing I just did. Draw a line across each picture of food. Do not draw a line across any other picture—just food. Go as fast as you can, but try not to make any mistakes. Let me know when you are finished. Are you ready? Go."** Time for 45 seconds. Do not allow your child to have an eraser. If he/she makes a mistake, tell him to just keep going. Write the completion time at the bottom of page 323. Check the responses with the answer key on the following pages.

Time: _____   # Correct _____

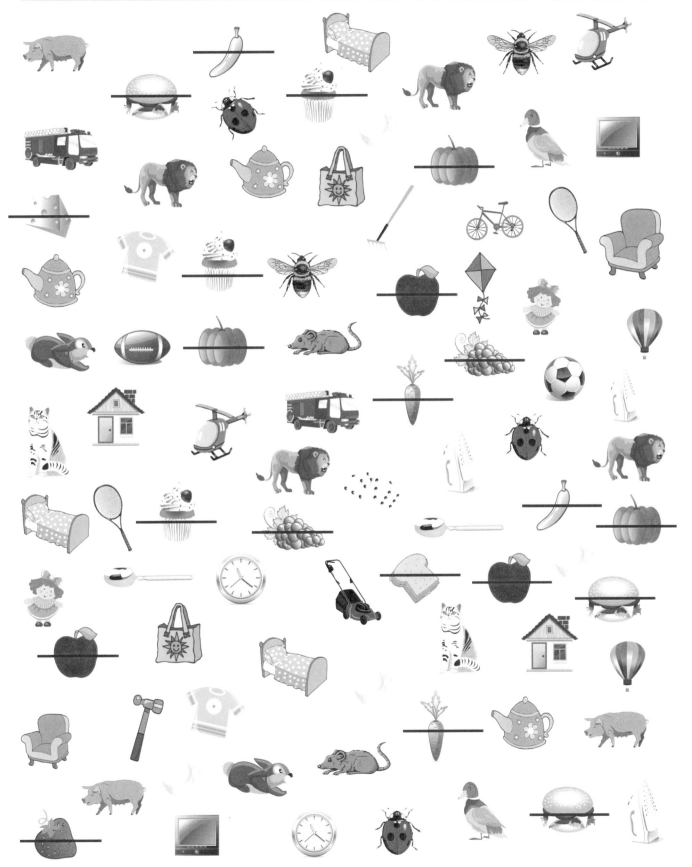

Exercise Instructions:
Say: **"Draw a line across each picture of food. Do not draw a line across any other picture—just food. Are you ready? Go."** Time for 45 seconds. Write the completion time at the bottom of page 327. Check the responses with the answer key on the following pages.

Time: _____   # Correct _____

Cancellation (Ordered)

CPSIA information can be obtained
at www.ICGtesting.com
Printed in the USA
BVRC100451030522
635566BV00002B/1